DAY CARE

SOURCE BOOKS
ON EDUCATION
(VOL. 12)

GARLAND REFERENCE LIBRARY
OF SOCIAL SCIENCE
(VOL. 360)

Source Books on Education

DAY CARE:
A Source Book

Kathleen Pullan Watkins
Lucius Durant, Jr.

WITHDRAWN

GARLAND PUBLISHING, INC. • NEW YORK & LONDON
1987

Library of Congress Cataloging-in-Publication Data

Watkins, Kathleen Pullan.
  Day care.

  (Garland reference library of social science ;
vol. 360. Source books on education ; vol. 12)
  Includes bibliographies and indexes.
  1. Child care services—United States. 2. Child
care services—United States—Bibliography. 3. Day
care centers—United States. 4. Day care centers—
United States—Bibliography. I. Durant, Lucius,
1932–   . II. Title. III. Series: Garland
reference library of social science ; v. 360.
IV. Series: Garland reference library of social science.
Source books on education ; v. 12.
HQ778.7.U6W38   1987   362.7′12   86-33548
ISBN 0-8240-8525-6 (alk. paper)

Printed on acid-free, 250-year-life paper
Manufactured in the United States of America

Lovingly Dedicated to Our Spouses

Gloria Dean Durant

and

Ronald Cleophus Watkins

CONTENTS

Section Three

Section Four

The purpose of this book is to provide the reader with an overview of the status, issues, and literature in the day care field. Despite an initial lack of public acceptance, today day care is one of the fastest growing areas in the United States. Unlike other trends in business and education, this is one field where growth is likely to continue well into the next century. Changes in the lifestyle and structure of American families, in particular the increasing numbers of working mothers and single parents, are among the factors influencing the need for child care alternatives.

Developing familiarity with the day care literature may be a task somewhat more difficult than in many other fields. The reasons for this dilemma are many. First, the language of day care and the regulations governing it vary considerably from state to state. Kinds of day care in wide use also vary depending upon the region of the country and locale in question. Second, day care personnel are an extremely diverse group. Some staff have had training to work with young children, while others have had little experience or preparation save that acquired as parents. Limited background can also mean that a child care worker lacks access to journals, periodicals, and organizations available within the field.

Sources of funding for day care are a third factor affecting the professional's familiarity with the literature. Non-profit programs may lack monies to make staff training, subscriptions, and conference attendance possible. When avenues for professional development continue to open-up, there are many individuals who are without access to information about the field. This volume is designed to provide both the professional and wide range of interested others with an introduction to the scope and direction of the day care community.

DAY CARE: A SOURCE BOOK includes several kinds of information. Introductory essays offer an overview of specific topics of interest. These are not intended to include all points of view, nor can this type of book provide examples of the many issues and problems discussed. Instead, these articles lead the reader to information to enable further investigation of the subjects described through the use of the annotated bibliographies which follow each of the essays. The bibliographies include books, journal articles, research reports, newspaper articles, and relevant brochures. A final section of this book lists many of the journals, periodicals, and newsletters available dealing with the concerns of day care professionals, providers, and clients. An attempt has been made to provide an up-to-date review of the literature, although volumes of significance have been included regardless of their date of publication.

This volume is organized in a manner to enable the reader to locate topics of special interest. Section One contains essays and bibliographies related to components of day care centers. Program administration and management, roles of child care workers, and components such as education, health, and social services are discussed in the first three essays. Essays on working with parents and program evaluation are also included in this section.

The second section of this book deals with kinds of day care and programs to meet specific needs. Articles on infant/toddler programs, family day care, and school-age child care are the segments of this part of the source book. Readers will note that employer-sponsored day care have not been accorded a separate essay. As this is not a widespread kind of program--nor does it appear there will be large numbers of such programs--day care as an employee benefit is dealt with in the third section of the book. This section deals with the many issues of concern to child care workers employed in day care. Professional development is dealt with in one article, and issues such as funding, regulation and sponsorship of programs are covered in another essay. The final segment of the book is devoted to a list of resources.

Selecting the bibliographic material for inclusion in this volume involved use of the following criteria: 1) Information is contemporary, representing accepted philosophy and child

development theory and programming practices. This criteria
also applied to older works with relevant viewpoints. 2) Information is relevant and applicable in multi-cultural settings
and without significant reference to practices or attitudes that
are regionalized or ethnic in nature. 3) Materials selected
portray day care as a field whose members are striving for acceptance of their professional status. Entries were avoided
which portrayed child care as babysitting. 4) Bibliographic in-
clusions reflect a wide range of issues, directions in the
field, and research findings. 5) The bulk of the entries contain information that is readable and useable by many of those
working in the field as well as those otherwise interested in
it. It was not the intention of the authors to limit reader-
ship to program developers and administrators. In fact, it is
our sincere hope that this presentation will stand as a statement of quality concerns and issues that will enlighten readers
and provide support for others already familiar with the field.

There are problems encountered in the writing of any book.
Two of these were of special significance to the authors.
First of all, no book can deal with every matter of importance
to readers. At one point, for example, it was suggested that
nannies, extended-family care, babysitters, and other in-home
child care should be included. These do not fall into the realm
of typical day care situations. They often include services to
or relationships with families that are not aspects of day care

provided in other settings. While several forms of in-home child care are mentioned they are not covered at length for these reasons.

A second problem involves the book's deadline. At some point the search for material ceases. This means that some information is omitted although it might be significant. The authors wish to assure readers that this was inadvertent, and every effort was made to secure appropriate, useful material for inclusion in this book.

The books, articles, and reports included in DAY CARE: A SOURCE BOOK were chosen to meet the needs of day care personnel, college faculty and students, community and business leaders, and parents interested in day care services. This diverse audience is the reason that information is provided in a readable, non-technical, and comprehensive style. It is our belief that the more individuals who find this volume useful, the greater the overall benefit to the day care community.

In some respects, this is a precarious time for the child care profession. It suffers from a lack of the organization so evident among workers in other human service fields. Its members are of extremely diverse backgrounds where training and experience are concerned. There are no uniform qualifications for day care staff across the United States. Furthermore, lax regulation of programs and personnel have made it possible for those interested primarily in financial gain, not children, to call themselves day care providers. Perhaps in some cases the care provided in these settings is adequate, but, we fear, in many it is substandard.

Finally, there are the day care opponents who uniformly condemn all care provided outside the home by those other than parents or extended family. There are the health care providers who believe that as a rule the conditions in day care centers are primitive and unsanitary. And there are those who are certain that every child in alternative care is in danger of molestation. These represent issues to be dealt with, challenges to be met. Awareness, familiarity with the literature is one of the tools which can be utilized to address these and future concerns of the day care community. The authors hope that this volume will be useful for just such purposes.

Our thanks, to all of those who have contributed to our knowledge of the field, especially our teachers, the late Drs. Evangeline Ward and Lois Macomber; to our families who provide unconditionally loving support; and to our editor and friend Marie Ellen Larcada.

Kathleen Pullan Watkins, Ed. D.
Lucius Durant, Jr., M. Ed.

GLOSSARY*

center-based day care - extended-day care provided for large groups of children in non-residential facilities, such as schools, recreation centers, or churches.

child care worker/caregiver/day care provider - terms used interchangeably in this volume to denote individuals working in direct service positions with children in day care settings.

child care/day care - terms used interchangeably in this volume to denote the range of programs and services providing custodial care and support for child development. It should be noted that "child care" is also used to describe a full range of special services to children in addition to day care.

family day care - extended-day care provided in the caregiver's own residence for small groups of children. In some states "group day care" describes care of a slightly larger group supervised by two or more caregivers, also in a private residence.

infant-toddler day care - extended-day care usually provided in group settings designed specifically for children in the age range from birth to three years.

school-age child care - programs or services to provide alternative care situations during the hours before and after school for children in the age range of six to twelve years.

---

*These definitions are provided by the authors for the purposes of clarity and continuity in this volume. It is recognized that terms may vary in different states or regions of the country.

Day Care

ADMINISTRATION AND MANAGEMENT OF DAY CARE CENTERS

For altruistic, social, spiritual, and economic reasons, from "love of children" to a convenient tax shelter, people are entering the child day care field in droves. According to some estimates, there are close to 40,000 centers across the United States providing some type of child care service.[1] Those in the profession believe such figures may be woefully inaccurate, given the suspected numbers of unlicensed and un-registered facilities. Whatever the actual numbers, the day care phenomenon is a significant distance from faddism. With statistics indicating that more than 50 percent of women with children under age six are employed outside the home,[2] the need for child care alternatives is increasing.

The demand for quality services, the sharp rise in the availability of slots, and recent media attention regarding sexual abuse by caregivers may be counted among the factors placing increasing pressure on day care providers. The pro-gram administrator's work is complicated by the fact that there is little training that adequately prepares an indivi-dual for the complexity of roles and responsibilities that

---

[1]U.S. Bureau of the Census, 1982.

[2]Lindsey, R. "Increased Demand for Day Care Prompts a Debate on Regulation," The New York Times, September 2, 1984, p. 52.

comprise the work of the center director. This chapter will explore the essential skills and unique roles played by the day care administrator and suggest some techniques useful in a director's professional growth plan.

The "Cultures" of Day Care

Today's educators have learned to borrow knowledge and skills from business and industry. Essential techniques and styles of management translate easily from the corporate to school settings and can maximize programmatic success.

For several years, one of the buzzwords of management training has been "culture."[3] This term has been used to identify the unique set of values, interactions, heroes, and other hallmarks characterizing an individual business. It is now recognized that the extent to which corporate culture is recognized and managed may play a major role in that business' realization of goals. We can speculate, even assume, that whenever a group of persons interact to achieve stated aims, a culture specific to that group will eventually evolve. Therefore, one of the roles of the day care center director

---

[3]Deal, T., and A. Kennedy. Corporate Cultures, Reading, Mass.: Addison-Wesley, 1982.

becomes the process of determining the features of that program's culture and then molding and using them to best advantage.

What factors influence a center's culture? Although in some ways they are similar to the determinants of corporate culture, in another sense education/human service settings present their own unique situations. For example, the staff and families who are participants in child care settings often come from the same community. This may mean that shared history, language, and values are already in place before a day care program becomes operational.

Another factor influencing day care center culture involves the environment created by program leadership. The director sets the tone for the manner in which personnel interact with one another, children, and parents. The director's utilization of staff expertise, their participation in decision-making, the clarity of program goals and objectives, and an open-door policy are the primary contributors to the environment.

While the internal milieu is vital to the nature of a center's culture, so is the environment in which the center is situated, that is, the neighborhood surrounding the facility and the climate in which the program exists. First, we have the immediate community which creates both a physical

and attitudinal setting for the center. Second, there is
the attitude of families and others toward day care services.
This can vary greatly from one parent to another. At one
time, family values were not terribly relevant to the survival of a program. Today, however, parents are increasingly
knowledgeable regarding child care choices, and many can
identify a high-quality program. With a growing number of
facilities available, directors must be better attuned to
what parents want for their children.

Culture is also determined by the values of a program,
which are set in place when the center is first established
and then evolve over time. These values are derived from the
program philosophy and goals. While on the surface, appropriate aims would seem enough, in actuality, the techniques
and leadership style used to meet short-term objectives speak
most clearly about the real values of program. If, for example, the program philosophy addresses the importance of
parent involvement, but the director actually discourages an
active role on the part of mothers and fathers, the action
outweighs the written goal statement.

Determining the components of day care center culture
is an ongoing task. It means advising everyone involved of
programmatic aims and means for achieving these. It means
becoming and staying attuned to the personal and professional

needs of staff and others affiliated with and utilizing services. It means monitoring the changing needs and priorities of the community to ascertain that the program remains in step with these. Perhaps most importantly, it means constant assessment of one's leadership role in the center, as the next section of this chapter will discuss.

Roles for Day Care Leaders

The human service professions make heavy demands upon administrators. We are not "pencil pushers" who merely shuffle papers, nor are we preoccupied with products. Instead, we are focused upon improving the quality of human growth and interaction. In the day care setting we are the facilitators of the overall development of young children and their families. In order to achieve this end, the roles of day care center administrators are broad and encompass the many needs of the adults and children involved in the program.

We have spoken already of the director as tone-setter, but another feature of this particular responsibility involves the administrator's position as role model. In so many ways the program's leader must demonstrate appropriate speech, dress, manner, and modes of interaction with others. Even in the area of professional growth, staff will take their cues from the behavior and attitudes of the director. If the administrator actively seeks means to add to his or her knowledge and skills via conference or college class attendance or professional readings and memberships, these activities become signals to other personnel that such engagements are considered time well spent. If, in addition, the director shares what is learned, staff are encouraged to do likewise.

Not insignificant among the roles of the day care administrator is that of interpreter of philosophy, policy, and procedures. Centers are beset by volumes of local, state, and federal regulations which must be strictly adhered to or licensure, funding, and other support may be in jeopardy. Without the support of leadership, the fundamental purpose of the program and roles of staff in relation to these may be in question. Policies which caregivers must interpret for parents, volunteers, and others must first be defined by the director. Especially important are the procedures outlined for handling unusual situations. If clearly delineated, these prevent many problems from arising and give staff a sense of security and direction.

A director is also responsible to the center's governing body (usually a board of directors or policy council) for the implementation of those policies, decisions, and fundamental components of the program. The achievement of goals hinges upon the statement of clear objectives and activities to meet them. At times, directors fail to include staff in

the program planning phase. This may result in a staff re-
sistant to policies and unaware of the impact of their lack
of cooperativeness. But can personnel be faulted if they
have not been shown how to function together to produce a
high quality program? Administrators cannot operate day care
programs alone. They must recognize and utilize staff potential and expertise. When staff are partners with the director in reaching for goals, all work toward the same ends in
a similar manner.

Because child care is a physically and emotionally tax-
ing kind of work, the program director often acts as <u>staff
counselor</u>. Although child care personnel are encouraged to
leave personal problems at home, emotional, family, and other
difficulties can interfere with the performance of a staff
member's responsibilities. Therefore, the administrator must
be willing to be a patient listener-supporter if it will help
a caregiver to resume his or her duties with the children.
Despite the fact that the counseling role can be invaluable,
the director must be cautious to keep administrative responsibilities firmly in mind. The tendency to be too empathetic
to staff problems can detract from the goals of the program.
The function of the director-counselor becomes one of helping the troubled staff member find temporary or permanent
solutions to outside problems, and then to refocus on caregiving tasks.

At times, the personnel problems that require supervisory counseling are those of the entire staff, rather than individual difficulties. Even the most cohesive staff members occasionally disagree and require a mediator to help restore unity. A day care administrator is well advised to keep lines of communication open, provide for stress relieving activities, and to work to prevent personnel problems from arising. If, despite considerable efforts, difficulties present themselves, a cool head and objective thinking are essential.

Qualities of Day Care Directors

Many researchers agree that there are three predominant styles of management. They are the "autocratic" (iron-fisted), the "laissez faire" (hands-off), and the democratic (let's vote) styles.[4] There is also agreement that the real manager is actually a compilation of all of these, presenting the style that best suits the situation. While this eclectic approach is probably ideal for day care directors, there are, nonetheless, qualities that are essential for effective management of child development centers.

Directors must first and foremost be knowledgeable about the operation of a day care center and about people.

---

[4]"Hildebrand, V. Management of Child Development Centers, New York: Macmillan Publishing Company, 1984, p. 114.

Unfortunately, such information is not often taught in teacher training institutions, but skills can be learned through life experience and observation of administrative role models. The evolution of this skill provides the information for informed decision making.

Willingness to accept responsibility and be involved in the decision-making process is a second important quality of day care directors. This process occurs at several levels in child care centers. There are decisions made solely by administrators without staff involvement. There are also decisions in which center personnel participate and in which the director acts as facilitator, providing information and guidelines. Yet another type of decision making involves the delegation of authority to qualified staff, parents, and others. No administrator can carry all the burdens of leadership; support is needed. Despite the fact that ultimate responsibility often rests with the director, that person must seek and promote the active involvement of responsible others in the decision making processes.

The value of a director's interpersonal skills is immeasurable. Sensitivity to a wide variety of needs and situations, even when those needs remain unspoken, is especially important. A keen ability to observe and respond appropriately to individuals and groups and knowledge of group dynamics is also crucial.

One of the key aspects of effective interpersonal skills is the ability to communicate with others. This involves listening, speaking, reading, and writing skills. A director must be able to utilize all available means to get across information to persons involved in the program and to communicate to those in the community what the program is about. The administrator learns to use staff meetings, one-to-one conferences, proposals, reports, letters, and memorandums to keep parents, staff, board members, and others up to date on programmatic developments. Being an effective communicator means evolving a clear, concise language, avoiding academic or professional jargon where inappropriate, and staying clear of any tendency to "talk down" to persons of a different economic, professional, or social status. When giving feedback to staff, a conscientious director avoids criticism that will trigger defense mechanisms and utilizes techniques that provide helpful suggestions and support for areas of strength.

Day care administrators must be possessed of strong planning and organizational skills. These skills run the gamut from simple to complex and from those permitting brainstorming to those demanding instantaneous decisions. Planning must be undertaken every working day under a set of guidelines that meet personal and professional needs. Director planning begins with the establishment of goals and a clear understanding of how administrative responsibilities fit into goal achievement. When planning is undertaken the director must work to achieve a balance between responsibilities to the professional community, staff, children and parents, and to self. This equilibrium is difficult, although not impossible, to achieve. One of the keys to effective planning is identifying priorities. Which tasks need to be undertaken first? Which can wait? Which tasks must be undertaken by the director and which can be delegated to others?

In light of their need to implement plans developed, directors must also be time managers and help themselves and others to use time effectively and productively. Some find it helpful to list each day's tasks in order of priority, along with a time frame for each task. Other administrators need to look closely at their daily schedules to determine the occasions and circumstances during which time can be used more effectively.

Day care center leaders should be well-balanced, well-rounded individuals who use work time for work projects yet recognize the value of leisure time and activities. When we first discovered the "burnout" syndrome, we discovered the workaholic. Dedication to job responsibilities is only as important as acknowledgement of personal needs for rest, recreation, and affection. Time must be made for stress-alleviating activities if a director is to produce at a consistently high-quality level. Day care interests and friendships must be developed, regular vacation or personal days taken, and time permitted for family needs and activities. Unfortunately, the director who is a workaholic often expects similar behavior from his or her staff. In turn, staff may become disgrunted and uncooperative if expected to give everything to their work. The director runs the risk of facilitating disloyalty, absenteeism, and apathetic attitudes.

Last, among important leadership skills, the day care administrator must be aware of the importance and uses of regular evaluation. Evaluation of program components, of staff, of environment, of children's progress, and of self is one of the most valuable tools a director has for improving the quality of the program. There are many measures of evaluation with which administrators should become familiar, including observation, standardized tests, questionnaires, staff projects, and home-school programs. Purpose of assessment and uses of information gathered must be considered prior to the selection of an evaluation device. A timetable for assessment must be developed.

The qualities and skills discussed are only some of the abilities needed by a day care director. Patience, humor, and other characteristics can help to lighten the administrative load considerably. Directors must themselves be developing persons, committed to the profession, the children and the families served. As we develop, Maslowe tells us, we eventually become "self-actualized."[5] With self-actualization come humility and the awareness that the more we know the more there is to learn. This may be the most important quality of any leader, for it promotes a lifelong interest in learning and stimulates the desire to facilitate and encourage the development of others.

---

[5]Maslowe, A. H. <u>Motivation and Personality</u>, New York: Harper and Row, 1954.

BIBLIOGRAPHY

Administration of Child Care Programs: Business Management.
    Lubbock, TX: Home Economics Curriculum Center, Texas
    Tech University, 1983.

    Curriculum for training the day care administrator in
the two-year college program. Topics include fiscal management, personnel management, and legal issues.

Breitbart, Vicki. The Day Care Book: The Why, What, and How
    of Community Day Care. New York: Knopf, 1977.

    A volume of techniques for developing child care pro-
grams in the community. Information included on a variety of
planning and implementation tasks, such as identifying sources
of funding, legal assistance, and members of the day care
policy board.

Brown, Janet F. (Ed.). Administering Programs for Young
    Children. Washington, DC: National Association for
    the Education of Young Children.

    A collection of articles from the journal, Young Chil-
dren, covering aspects of program administration. Topics
include programming, staff development, and health issues.

Cherry, Clare, Barbara Hunnes, and Kay Kaizma. Nursery School
    and Day Care Management Guide. Belmont, CA: Fearon-
    Pitman, 1978.

    A tabbed, binder edition of a day care administration
guide. Various aspects of program management are covered and
useful forms are provided. Even first aid is covered. Handy
for the director who wishes to later insert information on
administrative taks.

The Child Care Handbook. Washington, DC: American Home
    Economics Association, 1975.

    Provides for administrators and others an overview of
the issues and activities of day care programs. The need for
child care and contemporary influences on the profession are
described. Other topics discussed include licensing, business
and financing, child curriculum, health and safety, and working with parents.

Child Care Information Exchange, "The Changing World of the Child Care Director: Zolper Perspective: An Interview with Malcolm S. Host," <u>Child Care Information Exchange</u>, June 1984, pp. 21-23.

Historical perspective of the role, responsibilities, and challenges of the work of administering day care programs.

Clarke-Stewart, Alison. <u>Day Care</u>. Cambridge, MA: Harvard University Press, 1982.

Part of the Developing Child Series, this volume offers a brief history of day care, information on the current need for services, the roles and skills of caregivers. Looks at alternatives to the day care provided in the United States and Great Britain.

Click, Phyllis. <u>Administration of Schools for Young Children</u>, Second Edition. Albany, NY: Delmar Publishers, Inc., 1981.

This volume includes a section on administrators' professional growth and legal responsibilities, in addition to chapters addressing program planning and operation. Parent education and involvement, as well as suggestions for public relations techniques are also covered.

Cohen, Donald J. <u>Day Care: 3 Serving Preschool Children</u>. U.S. Department of Health, Education, and Welfare, Office of Human Development, Office of Child Development, 1975.

An overview of all the facets and components of day care services, including facilities utilized, parent involvement, health, psychosocial, and consultation services. Models of center-based care and program networks are described.

"Consulting as a Cure for Director Burnout," <u>Child Care Information Exchange</u>, September 1980, pp. 18-22.

These are a compilation of suggestions from day care directors designed to provide outlets for skills and tensions. Helps the reader to determine whether he or she has the skills, personality, and expertise to function in a consultant capacity. Potential opportunities for consultant jobs as well as suggestions to assure success are provided.

Deal, Terence E., and Allen A. Kennedy. <u>Corporate Cultures: The Rites and Rituals of Corporate Life</u>. Reading, MA: Addison-Wesley Publishing Company, 1982.

A book that caused a revolution in the business world. Explores the values, heroes, and communication systems at work when people work together in groups. Can provide new insight into those factors affecting human interaction in the day care setting.

Decker, Celia Anita, and John R. Decker. Planning and Administering Early Childhood Programs, Third Edition. Columbus, OH: Charles E. Merrill Publishing Company, 1984.

Provides a rationale for appropriate administration of early childhood programs. Emphasis is placed on developing a philosophical foundation upon which programs may be based. Topics covered include development of policies and procedures, staffing programs, planning and scheduling children's programs, and handling financial matters.

Early Childhood Directors Association of St. Paul, MN. Survival Kit for Directors. St. Paul, MN: Toys 'n Things Press, 1984.

Contributions from 95 program directors regarding solutions to common problems experienced in the day care milieu.

Frank, Mary, and Bettye Caldwell. Marketing Child Care Programs: Why and How, New York: Haworth Press, 1985.

Case studies and techniques for the successful marketing of day care programs. Frank discussion of resistance to this issue and obstacles to marketing.

Greenman, James T., and Robert W. Fugua (Eds.). Making Day Care Better: Training, Evaluation, and the Process of Change. New York: Teachers College Press, 1984.

Status of the child care profession and suggestions for stimulating the change process in staff environments, and other areas. Contributions from many professionals in the field. Divided into three parts covering, "The Ecology of Day Care," "Unraveling Outcomes," and "Changing Day Care."

Grossman, Bruce D., and Carol Keyes. Early Child Administration. Boston: Allyn and Bacon, Inc., 1985.

Devotes opening chapters to aspects of creating an early childhood center. Emphasizes the humanistic approach to administration and meeting family and staff needs. Examines the various roles of directors, including the advocacy role in relation to children, families, and staff.

Harragan, Betty Lehan. Games Mother Never Taught You: Cor-
     porate Gamesmanship for Women. New York: Warner Books,
     Inc., 1977.

     Identifies for women administrators some of the unwritten
rules of the business world. Focuses on those interpersonal
skills and human interactions the author considers typical of
the corporate setting. Helpful for the day care administrator
active in the business community or pursuing federal or foundation funds.

Hewes, Dorothy W. (Ed.). Administration: Making Programs
     Work for Children and Families. Washington, DC:
     National Association for the Education of Young Chil-
     dren, 1979.

     Contents include essays on the development of goals and
objectives, principles of management, staff development,
family problems, and program evaluation. Contributors are
from a multi-disciplinary group of educators, health care
professionals, and other fields.

Hewes, Dorothy W., and Barbara Hartman. Early Childhood Ad-
     ministration: A Workbook for Administrators. San
     Francisco: R and E Research Associates, 1979.

     Management theory and principles applied to the day care
setting. Workbook style chapters on determination of goals,
working with staff and community, and program evaluation.

Hildebrand, Verna. Management of Child Development Centers.
     New York: Macmillan Publishing Company, 1984.

     Suggests an "ecological system framework" for the man-
agement of programs for young children. Emphasizes management principles for leadership, financial aspects, and health
and safety components of child care programs. An interesting
feature are samples of decisions faced by administrators which
provide a basis for discussion of problem solving and effective managerial techniques.

Host, Malcolm S., and Pearl B. Heller. Administration.
     Washington, DC: U.S. Office of Health, Education, and
     Welfare, Office of Child Development, 1971.

     An older but still relevant volume on administration.
Organization, components, and management of day care centers
are covered. Useful forms are provided.

"How to Start a Child Care Center," Report on Preschool Programs, Special Report, June 11, 1986.

Outcome of a 1986 conference on child day care. Describes how to conduct a needs assessment, processes for securing funding, identifying a facility, budgeting, obtaining liability insurance, and staffing a program.

Lombardo, Victor S., and Edith Foran Lombardo. Developing and Administering Early Childhood Programs. Springfield, IL: Charles C. Thomas, Publisher, 1983.

Presents the roles and tasks of the administrators of programs for young children. Much emphasis is placed on the characteristics of youngsters and the process of developing programs to meet their needs.

McMurphy, John R. Day Care and Preschool Handbook for Churches. Chappaqua, NY: Christian Herald Books, 1981.

Deals with the unique situation presented by the church-sponsored day care center. Administration, program planning and operation, and leadership all within the framework of the religious preschool philosophy are discussed.

Morgan, Gwen G. Managing the Day Care Dollars. St. Paul, MN: Toys 'n Things Press, 1982.

Financial planning, accounting procedures for the day care director. Sample forms, worksheets are provided. Designed for those with little previous budget and accounting experience.

Neugebauer, Roger, "Are You an Effective Leader?," Child Care Information Exchange, January 1979, pp. 5-12.

Four types of leaders are described and a leadership assessment tool is provided to enable directors to self-study their skills in the areas of planning, decision-making, communications. Useful for the director interested in professional growth.

Neugebauer, Roger, "Staff Selection: Choosing the One from the Many," Child Care Information Exchange, Summer, 1978, pp. 3-11.

Describes the complete process for hiring day care staff, including selection and training of personnel committee members, screening resumes, and questioning applicants.

Rogolsky, Maryrose, "Psychologist Views the Role of a Day
     Care Director," Child Care Information Exchange, Sep-
     tember 1979, pp. 1-5.

     A discussion of the emotional impact of administrative
roles in day care. Feelings of loneliness, isolation,
stress, and the extent of director responsibilities are described. Supervisory problems are called the "greatest
problem" faced by directors. Suggestions are provided to
enable administrators to meet personal needs for support.

Schon, Bruce, "Director's Survival Kit: Marketing," Child
     Care Information Exchange, May 1981, pp. 17-24.

     Complete information on techniques to market a day care
program including logo design, brochure development, gener-
ating publicity.

Sciarra, Dorothy June and Anne G. Dorsey. Developing and
     Administering a Child Care Center. Boston: Houghton
     Mifflin, 1979.

     A day care administration volume designed for those
without previous directing experience. Topics covered include the selection of site, equipment and materials, staffing the program, and health and safety issues.

Seaver, Judith W., and Carol A. Cartwright. Child Care
     Administration. Belmont, CA: Wadsworth Publishing
     Company, 1986.

     An extensive exploration of many aspects of day care
administration. Discusses various types of programs and
issues related to designing and managing each. Excellent
resources follow each chapter. A highly recommended volume.

Secor, Christine Dimock. Handbook for Day Care Board Members,
     Revised Edition. New York: Day Care Council of New
     York, Inc., 1984.

     Covers starting a program, organizing a board and work-
ing with members, fund raising, and legal issues. A how-to
for board members and directors who work with policy board
input.

Stevens, Joseph H., Jr., and Edith W. King. Administering
     Early Childhood Education Programs. Boston: Little,
     Brown and Company, Inc., 1976.

One of the earlier volumes dealing with early childhood administration. Provides overviews of the history and theory predominant in the field. Reviews research conducted up to 1976. Examines roles of parents, staff, and support services in the preschool program.

Storm, S. The Human Side of Child Care Administration: A How-To Manual. Washington, DC: National Association for the Education of Young Children, 1986.

Guidelines for the new administrator in the day care setting provided in a binder format. Focuses on interpersonal communications issues, including development of personnel policies, recruiting, motivating, and assessing staff performance. Problem solving strategies are also discussed.

Struts, Donald T. (Ed.). Administering Day Care and Preschool Programs. Boston: Allyn and Bacon, Inc., 1982.

Compilation of articles on aspects of administration by experts in the field. Discusses planning, staffing, fiscal management, among other topics.

Travis, Nancy, and Joe Perreault. Day Care Personnel Management. Atlanta, GA: Southern Regional Education Board, 1979.

Discussion of aspects of hiring, supervising, compensating, and evaluating day care staff. Federal legislation related to personnel is covered. Suggestions are provided for motivating employees.

Watkins, Kathleen Pullan, and Lucius Durant, Jr. The Early Childhood Director's Staff Development Handbook. Englewood Cliffs, NJ: Prentice-Hall, Inc., 1987.

A complete overview of the staff development and training processes. Includes chapters on needs assessment, planning training activities, using consultants, and evaluating staff development activities. A variety of sample forms and other workbook-style activities are provided.

Yocum, Jan C., Donna Franzell, and Gloria C. Simms. How to Start a Day Care Center. Washington, DC: Day Care and Child Development Council of America, 1981.

Step-by-step process to starting a day care center with emphasis on day care as a business. Bibliographies are provided to address additional reader questions.

ROLES AND RESPONSIBILITIES OF TEACHERS AND CAREGIVERS

Since the dawn of the American "day nursery"[1] at the end of the nineteenth century, the child care worker has suffered from a long identity crisis. First a custodian, then a social worker, then a babysitter, the caregiver seems at last to be coming to public attention as a highly skilled, trained professional. The development of college training programs, the awarding of teacher certification for the nursery school level, the formation of professional associations, and the creation of the Child Development Associate Credential[2] each provided valuable assists in the professionalization process. Even now, however, the vast majority of day care personnel lacks appropriate education and credentials.

Perhaps the greatest hurdle to overcome, however, is one yet to be surmounted. That is, a change must occur in the thinking of the general public about the child care profession. Many people still believe that it takes no special skills to care for young children. In most states, although one must be licensed to be a hair stylist or to sell real estate, an individual needs no credentials to provide day care services.

---

[1]Steinfels, Margaret O'Brien. Who's Minding the Children. New York: Simon and Schuster, 1973, p. 34.

[2]The Child Development Associate Program: A Guide to Training, Second Edition. Washington, DC: U.S. Government Printing Office, Fall 1981.

Meanwhile, within the field there is a growing air of professionalism and awareness of the unique contributions of day care providers, as well as those skills and characteristics which are marks of high quality caregiving. As the day care concept emerged from its custodial-care confines and blossomed into the child and family development program of today, the role of the caregiver was acknowledged to be more important. As research illustrated the importance of the child's earliest years, and the facets of the "whole" child emerged, day care centers began to develop components to address and facilitate physical, cognitive, and social-emotional competence. It was no longer adequate to think of early childhood programs as mere promoters of socialization and creative expression. Correspondingly, the caregiver became the child development specialist, curriculum planner, and family consultant of today.

Despite an increasing demand for trained personnel, many entry-level caregivers are young high school graduates, while others are housewives seeking a return to the job force.[3] Even those persons who possess both education and experience find that each day care program presents a unique situation created by the administration, staff, families, and the community served. Therefore, program directors must be active

---

[3]Nadel, Ruth G. "Training for Child Care Work: Project Fresh Start," Washington, DC: U.S. Department of Labor, Women's Bureau, 1979.

in the process of helping caregivers to recognize, accept, and fulfill the broad range of developing responsibilities.

Caregiving roles are influenced by a variety of factors. For the sake of brevity it may be helpful to look at these as emanating from three primary sources: administration, family, and community.

Administration consists of the director and advisory board or council of the center. Essentially, the people who develop policy and interpret legal issues for the program constitute the administration. In some centers, another member of the administrative-supervisory team is the head teacher, who has overall control of curriculum development.[4]

The responsibilities of staff are first outlined in the job descriptions prepared by the director. A caregiver is usually made familiar with these at the time of hiring. Written descriptions of caregiving responsibilities, however, are seldom the sole determinants of the roles of individual child care workers. If a director sets clear goals and creates a tone of cooperation, staff responsibilities often cross formal lines, and each caregiver attends to whatever tasks are present. When staff are encouraged to develop professionally, child care workers tend to treat their responsibilities with

---

[4]This is true when the director does not have early childhood, child care, or child development background.

creativity, seeking new levels of involvement in their
work.

Also influenced is the center's policy board. Where the
input of staff is sought, respected, and utilized, personnel
are more likely to facilitate, rather than thwart, the implementation of program policies. In this fashion, staff are
partners with administration in helping to establish the
philosophy of the center through their interaction with one
another, with families served, and with community members.

Families are the second of the factors affecting the
roles of caregivers. Through their interactions with staff,
parents help to identify such family needs as a safe and
healthy environment for their child during adult working
hours. But parents often provide much additional information.
They let their child's caregiver know in many ways what they
want for their youngster, both for the short-term and for the
child's future. At times this information is given very directly, but usually staff glean parental hopes and ideas
through a mother's and father's interactions with or conver-
sations about their youngster. Parental needs must not only
be respected but also play a part in how caregivers plan for,
relate to, and evaluate children's progress. For example,
some parents encourage the growth of surrogate-parent type
relationships between their child and the center staff, a role
not necessarily supported by professionals. Other parents

have strong beliefs about their own role as their youngster's primary caregiver. These families feel that too great an involvement on the part of a child care worker may threaten or interfere with their interactions with their child. Thus, a caregiver watches, listens, and is influenced by the parents' interpretation of their responsibilities.

The third influence on caregiving roles and responsibilities is the community. "Community" may be interpreted in two different ways. There is the physical community in which the center is located and to which the day care program is a contributing member. There is also the community spirit, a larger, somewhat less tangible entity. It is the latter definition that determines the amount of acceptance and status that the child care worker has.

To understand the great impact of this second aspect of community, let us consider two different types of situations common to day care professionals. If a center exists in an area where training and certification of staff and membership in professional organizations are not common, then community attitudes toward child care staff may reflect a lack of understanding of the value of day care and the roles of caregivers. If, on the other hand, the physical community offers varied opportunities for caregiver professional development, and if many centers compete to provide high-quality day care, then the service consumers (parents) tend to be more aware of the qualifications for the skills of caregivers. In other words, the community's interpretation of caregiving responsibilities will be one which values the work of day care providers.

But what specifically are the roles played by child care workers? To answer this question the same three criteria may be utilized as when discussing the influencing factors. In the broad framework of child care responsibilities, some are in relation to other staff and program administration, some deal with children and families; some are the result of community interaction; and still others meet needs for personal and professional growth.

The primary role of a caregiver in relation to co-workers is that of membership on the caregiving team. Implied in this partnership are the responsibilities of team loyalty, maintenance of communication, establishment of shared goals, and the sharing of experiences and new information.[5] The role of team member is a critical one upon which a second role hinges, that of implementer of administrative policies and decisions. Much of the success of this role depends upon caregivers' understanding of policies and

---

[5]Watkins, Kathleen P., and Lucius Durant, Jr. "Developing Professional Partnerships in Early Childhood Education Settings," Target I, Amarillo, TX: Teaching Pathways, Inc., 1983.

the freedom they have to carry out those policies. Child care workers require clear lines of command and support in order to form and maintain cohesive, harmonious teams to achieve the aims of the program.

The interactions of caregivers with children and their parents should always be guided by knowledge of the important roles played in relation to those persons. Child care workers are the planners, implementers, and evaluators of children's activities and progress. This function is especially important in the extended day program, as it permits the worker to play his or her second role--facilitator of children's overall growth and development. Caregiving teams must work cooperatively to conduct regular assessments of children's needs and provide experiences and activities to fill them. To achieve this end, regular team meetings and planning sessions are essential. In the implementation process, child care workers observe, interact, promote using the prepared environment, appropriate equipment and materials, and directed, purposeful involvement to stimulate the development of each child.

Day care personnel play a vital role as models for both children and their parents. Children observe and imitate the language and behavior of their teachers. Caregivers help youngsters to learn the purpose and benefits of listening to directions, sharing, cooperation, and observing rules. While many child care workers are conscientious during adult-child interactions, some are less aware of their behavior when conversing with co-workers. It is at these times that although children seem preoccupied by play, they are actually listening intently and watching the adults around them.

Workers at day care centers have the unique opportunity to influence parents' interactions with their children. As the child care worker has gradually been identified as a specialist, parents have begun to utilize their youngsters' teachers as resources. With the virtual disappearance of the extended family, mothers and fathers have fewer support systems. In addition to the many stresses of a highly technological and depersonalized society, parents often find themselves alone with childrearing problems during the critical early years. Child care workers are gradually stepping into roles that combine modeling for parents, information giving, and the provision of a supportive, structured, family-oriented environment.

In a variety of situations and circumstances, child care workers come into contact with the community. They have many opportunities to familiarize family, friends, and neighbors with the day care center and its functioning. A surprising number of people who never had any experience with child care have serious misconceptions about the purpose and values of day care. Such perceptions can often be changed by a responsible caregiver representative.

Perhaps the most important of the roles played by the caregiver in the community is that of child and family advocate. A child care worker must recognize, speak out about, and attempt to address issues on behalf of children and their parents, even those unrelated to day care services. Despite the establishment of children's rights and changes in the legal system designed to protect families, many problems need the strong support or intervention of the child advocate. Membership and participation in advocacy groups is an important caregiving role.

Child care workers are themselves members of families, fulfilling roles as sons, daughters, husbands, wives, and parents. Although, as professionals, caregivers seek to separate home and work lives, there must also be a healthy balance between the two. All of the life roles played by an individual are merely facets of a single person, and all aspects of self must be stimulated to grow and develop. If a single facet stagnates, the other parts will eventually suffer.

A caregiver can control and strongly influence the growth of the professional self. One of the most valuable ways to achieve this end is for a caregiver to work in a day care center where staff development is a priority. In such a program, the director seeks many opportunities for the growth of personnel. Individual staff talents and expertise are recognized and utilized, and caregivers provide input in the decision-making process. But even without a strong staff development component, caregivers have options for professional growth. There are early childhood organizations to join, journals and periodicals to read, conferences and workshops to attend. Furthermore, when ideas and information are brought back to the center and shared, the partnership among staff members is strengthened and all benefit.

The day care profession is a young and growing one, and many of those in the field are dedicated and enthusiastic. While the researchers and scholars make important contributions, it is those who work every day with children and families, the caregivers, who truly make the difference. American families will increasingly need child care services, and the interdisciplinary roles of the caregiver will continue to expand and develop. If the highest quality services are to be offered, the potential scope of those roles must be recognized, nurtured, and valued by program administrators, parents, the public, but primarily by caregivers themselves.

BIBLIOGRAPHY

Adler, Jack. Fundamentals of Group Child Care: A Textbook
    and Instructional Guide for Child Care Workers. Cam-
    bridge, MA: Ballinger, 1981.

    Contains information on a variety of practice issues,
historical perspectives on group care, and theoretical bases.
Effective chapters on tasks of caregivers and on child dis-
ciplines.

Beaty, Janice J. Skills for Preschool Teachers, Second Edi-
    tion. Columbus, OH: Charles E. Merrill Publishing
    Company, 1984.

    A unique volume which utilizes the Child Development
Associate competencies and functional areas as the framework for training teachers/caregivers who work with young
children. Each chapter focuses on a different functional
area and is followed by suggestions for portfolio entries
and an evaluation sheet to be used by the trainer.

Boressoff, Todd. Children, the Early Childhood Classroom
    and You: A Guide for Students and Volunteer Assistants.
    New York: Early Childhood Council of New York City,
    1983.

    Contains descriptions of the characteristics of young
children and the roles of those who come into contact with
them in early childhood settings. This volume contains
suggestions for volunteers to utilize during many parts of
the day and in various interest centers.

Bowerat, Roberta Wong. A Survey of State Certification
    Requirements of Teachers of Young Children from State
    Teacher Certification Offices and A Survey of Recog-
    nition Systems from Non-Governmental Organizations.
    Washington, DC: National Association for the Educa-
    tion of Young Children, 1983.

    Describes state-by-state positions on early childhood
certification, requirements for certification, and the
certifying state offices or agencies. States accepting the
Child Development Associate Credential and other forms of
professional recognition for teachers of young children are
also listed. A list of recommendations for additional research and professional policy follows.

Brawley, Edward A., Helene Gerstein, and Kathleen M. Watkins, "A Competency-Based Training Program for Day Care Personnel," Child Care Quarterly, Vol. 10, No. 2, Summer 1981, pp. 125-136.

The development and results of a competency-based training program which served 75 child day care and preschool personnel at the Community College of Philadelphia are described. Program is based upon the Child Development Associate competencies and prepared trainees for CDA assessment.

Busch-Rossnagel, Nancy A., and Barbara Meade Worman, "A Comparison of Educators' and Providers' Rankings of Important Competencies for Day Care Professionals," Child Care Quarterly, Vol. 14, No. 1, Spring 1985, pp. 56-71.

This research study consisted of the ranking by child care professionals of those competencies they considered most important for work with children in the day care setting. The authors expanded on the Child Development Associate competencies to include those specific to various job levels. Personal Qualities, Management, Staff Relations were among the identified skills areas for directors. Teachers rated promotion of children's emotional development the highest for the competency areas.

CDA Candidate's Local Assessment Team Book. Washington, DC: U.S. Department of Health and Human Services, Office of Human Development Services, Administration for Children, Youth and Families, Head Start Bureau, 1981.

Guidelines for the candidate applying for the Child Development Associate credential regarding assessment process. Descriptions of the roles and responsibilities of the members of the Local Assessment Team (LAT) and procedures for the Team meeting are discussed.

Chaklos, Linda R. USAFE Child Care Training Guide. Arlington, VA: ERIC Document Reproduction Service, 1981.

Training guide for caregivers in the United States Air Forces in Europe. Emphasis on uses of activity centers, such as library corner, dramatic play area, art, blocks, music, and water and sand play. Some information is included on child development and caregiver roles and relationships.

Child Care Helper Program: A Guide for Program Leaders.
     New York: Early Adolescent Helper Program, Graduate
     School and University Center of the City University of
     New York, 1985.

     Presents curriculum for preteens training to work as
child care aides with preschool age children. Might also
be used in elementary and secondary parenting education programs or child development courses.

Cinnane, Patrick, "A Man in Child Care - Contrast and Con-
     tradiction," Child Care Information Exchange, July/
     August 1981, pp. 1-4.

     The rewards and problems associated with being a male
caregiver.

Conger, Flora Stabler, and Irene B. Rose. Child Care Aide
     Skills. New York: McGraw-Hill Book Company, 1979.

     A training volume which focuses on the many aspects of
caregiving. An overview of the profession is provided.
Skills needed for work with various age groups, infant-
toddlers, preschoolers, and school-age children are discussed. Features sections on projects, issues and "what
would you do if...."

Fane, Xenia F. Child Care Careers. Englewood Cliffs, NJ:
     Prentice-Hall, Inc., 1977.

     From entry level to management level this volume dis-
cusses some of the choices in child care careers, such as
early childhood education, center-based and family day care.
Suggestions for finding the right position and going through
the interview process are included. Case studies of child
care personnel add a personal note.

Goldman, Richard, and Leo Anglin, "Evaluating Your Care-
     givers: Four Observation Systems," Day Care and Early
     Education, Fall 1979, pp. 40-41.

     Provides suggestions for four systems of observing day
care personnel: an anthropological format, counting specific behaviors, time sampling, and verbatim techniques.
Stresses that effective administration is the key to assuring quality interactions in day care environments.

Gordon, Tom, and Thomas W. Draper, "Sex Bias Against Male Workers in Day Care," Child Care Quarterly, Vol. 11, No. 3, Fall 1982, pp. 215-217.

Attitudinal responses to male caregivers are described as factors in high turnover rates among male caregivers. Need for changes in professional, parental, and public views of male caregivers is cited.

Gould, Nora Palmer, "Caregivers in Day Care: Who Are They?," Day Care and Early Education, Vol. 10, No. 4, Summer 1983, pp. 17.

Provides the results of a survey of child care professionals in Duchess County, New York. Characteristics of directors, teachers, and aides are described, including sex, education, hours worked daily, salary, and other factors.

Greenberg, Polly. Day Care Do-It-Yourself Staff Growth Program. Washington, DC: The Growth Program, 1975.

A large volume designed to provide a training curriculum for day care and other preschool personnel. Child curriculum development and child health and safety are among the topics covered.

Hernandez-Logan, Carmela (Ed.). Caregiving: A Multidisciplinary Approach. Palo Alto, CA: R and E Research Associates, 1981.

A discussion by practitioners of the roles and issues in various caregiving positions of human and health services providers, including day care personnel and nurses.

Hess, Robert D., and Doreen J. Croft. Teachers of Young Children. Boston: Houghton Mifflin, 1981.

A teacher-training text which provides practical examples and applications of theoretical principles. Setting goals for children and various administrative tasks are discussed, as well as curriculum areas traditional in early childhood education.

Hostetler, Lana and Edgar Klugman, "Early Childhood Job Titles: One Step Toward Professional Status," Young Children, Vol. 37, No. 6, September 1982.

Describes the impact of certain child care/early education job titles on perceptions of their corresponding skills and job responsibilities. Suggests that job titles and descriptions be rewritten for the Directory of Occupational Titles by the Department of Labor as one method to begin to elevate the recognition, salary, and benefits of early childhood educators.

Jackson, Brian, and Sonia Jackson. Childminder: A Study in Action Research. London: Routledge and Kegan Paul, 1979.

A study of British family day care providers with recommendations applicable in the United States. Suggests special training programs and a charter for home care workers.

Jones, Leroy, Sarah B. Hardy, and Diane H. Rhodes. The Child Development Associate Program: A Guide to Program Administration. Washington, DC: U.S. Department of Health and Human Services, Office of Human Development Services, 1981.

Provides a history of the Child Development Associate Consortium and discussion of the administration and funding of the program. The processes by which training monies are awarded and services delivered are described.

Kasindorf, Mary Eitingon. Competencies: A Self Guide to Competencies in Early Childhood Education. Atlanta, GA: Humanics Ltd., 1980.

A complete tool for educator self-assessment and development in the six competency areas described by the Child Development Associate Credentialing Program. Each of the CDA functional areas is described and self-check lists, bibliographies, and activities to promote teacher competence are provided.

Katz, Lilian G. Talks with Teachers: Reflections on Early Childhood Education. Washington, DC: National Association, 1977.

Discusses the stages of teacher development. Emphasis is placed on the unique growth processes and problems of early childhood educators. The development of the teacher is also viewed within the framework of children's growth needs.

<u>A Lap to Sit On and Much More - Help for Day Care Workers</u>.
Wheaton, MD: Association for Childhood Education International, 1971.

A classic collection of articles covering issues related
to the roles of caregivers and other early childhood educators working with young children. From issues of the journal
<u>Childhood Education</u>.

Lay-Dopyera, Margaret, and John Dopyera. <u>Becoming a Teacher</u>
<u>of Young Children</u>, Second Edition. Lexington, MA:
Heath Books, 1982.

A skills development for those interested in work with
young children. Focuses also on describing various philosophical and practical approaches to child development.
The characteristics of effective early childhood educators
are discussed.

Lero, Donna S., "Needed: Standard Policies on Reporting Suspected Child Abuse in Day Care and Preschool Centers,"
<u>Journal of Child Care</u>, Vol. 1, No. 3, January 1983, pp.
77-85.

Discusses the obligations of caregivers when child abuse
is suspected. Points out that many suspected cases of abuse
are not reported and which factors are believed responsible.
Urges that programs develop policies around all child abuse
issues.

Machado, Jeanne M., and Helen C. Meyer. <u>Early Childhood</u>
<u>Practicum Guide: A Sourcebook for Beginning Teachers</u>
<u>of Young Children</u>. Albany, NY: Delmar Publishers
Inc., 1984.

Presents the factors at play and roles of the practicum
student in relation to programming for children, development
of communication skills, observing and planning for children,
working with parents and volunteers, and development of teaching competencies. Suggestions for job search techniques are
also included.

Neugebauer, Roger, "Planning for Infant Care: The Care and
Finding of Infant Caregivers," <u>Child Care Information</u>
<u>Exchange</u>, September 1978, pp. 1-6.

Guidelines for selecting staff for infant care positions.
Tips for promoting high quality performance and maintaining
morale and sense of job satisfaction are included.

Neugebaurer, Roger, "Planning for Infant Care: Training
    Techniques for Better Caregiving. Child Care Informa-
    tion Exchange, November 1978, pp. 25-28.

This article provides guidelines for staff training of
persons working with infants and toddlers. Techniques for
training are discussed in detail, such as apprenticeships,
observations, problem solving, and child studies.

"New Methods for Educating and Credentialing Professionals
    in Child Care: The Child Development Associate Pro-
    gram," Child Quarterly, Vol. 10, No. 1, Spring 1981.

An entire issue of Child Care Quarterly devoted to key
issues in the training, assessment, and credentialing processes. History and critical evaluation of the importance of
the Child Development Associate Credential are provided.

Ornstein, Allan C., Harriet Talmage, and Anne W. Juhasz.
    The Paraprofessionals Handbook: A Guide for the
    Teacher-Aide. Belmont, CA: Fearon, 1975.

Guidelines for the basics in working as a teacher as-
sistant in the classroom. Addresses topics such as child
development, discipline issues, and interactions with co-
workers.

Peterson, Karen L., and Joan E. Raven, "Guidelines for Super-
    vising Student Teachers," Child Care Information Ex-
    change, September/October 1983, pp. 27-29.

Stages observed by directors in the development of student teachers. Roles of supervisors in the facilitation of
student development.

Scavo, Marlene, et al. The "Caring" Role in a Child Care
    Center. Staff Development Series, Military Child Care
    Project. Washington, DC: Office of the Assistant Sec-
    retary of Defense for Manpower and Reserve Affairs,
    April 1982.

Three volumes covering various aspects of caregiving
roles. Volume I: Staff Orientation; Volume II: Relating to
Parents; Volume III: Relating to Children.

Scavo, Marlene, et al. Staff Development Series, Military
    Child Care Project. Washington, DC: Office of the
    Assistant Secretary of Defense for Manpower and Reserve
    Affairs, April 1982.

Four volumes each devoted to the responsibilities and activities of caregivers in military child care facilities. Volumes cover Caring for School-Age Children, Caring for Preschoolers, Caring for Toddlers, Caring for Pretoddlers.

Schwebel, Andrew I., et al. The Student Teacher's Handbook: A Step-by-Step Guide Through the Term. New York: Barnes and Noble, 1979.

A study of the student-teaching experience designed to aid those involved. Using excerpts from student teaching logs readers are encouraged to develop realistic attitudes toward work in the classroom and skills for responding appropriately to day-to-day problems.

Snow, Charles W., "In-Service Day Care Training Programs: A Review and Analysis," Child Care Quarterly, Vol. 11, No. 2, Summer 1982, pp. 108-121.

A comparison of fourteen in-service training programs. Sponsorship, goals, content, methods, and evaluation are examined. Implications are derived for development of additional programs.

Todd, Vivian Edminston. The Aide in Early Childhood Education. New York: Macmillan Publishing Company, Inc., 1973.

Describes the roles of aides in the areas of helping children learn daily routines and reinforcing children's concepts. Some emphasis on developing competencies and the professional growth of the aide.

Vander Ven, Karen, Martha A. Mattingly, and Marian G. Morris, "Principles and Guidelines for Child Care Personnel Preparation Programs," Child Care Quarterly, Vol.11, No. 3, Fall 1982, pp. 221-244.

Describes the products of the Conference-Research Sequence in Child Care Education. Presents guidelines, educational, curricula, and field practice, for those involved in planning and implementing training programs. Proposes an agenda for future research in the child care field.

Washburn, Paul V., and Judith Sostarich Washburn, "The Four Roles of the Family Day Care Provider," Child Welfare, Vol. LXIV, No. 5, Sept.-Oct. 1985, pp. 547-554.

The authors distinguish four primary roles of family day care providers: nursery school teacher, foster or substitute parent, custodian, and businessperson. A table of skills rated most important by providers is included.

Wilson, La Visa Cam, and Neith Headley. <u>Working With Young Children</u>. Wheaton, MD: Association for Childhood Education International, 1983.

Provides an introduction to care of children in centers. Roles for caregivers in day care and early childhood settings are discussed.

COMPONENTS OF DAY CARE PROGRAMS

Until the 1960s, views of the competence of young children were extremely limited. Youngsters were treated as if
the capacity for learning was activated by entrance into
kindergarten or first grade. Except for the rare theorist,
researcher, or educator, few workers in the field placed significant value on the development that occurred before age
five.

Today, however, we speak of educating the "whole child"[1]
from birth. The earliest experiences are known to have an
impact on the infant. The roles played by parents, other
caretakers, and subsidiary attachment figures are stressed,
as they facilitate or inhibit growth in early childhood.

The day care center has become the home-away-from-home
for many preschool children. By some estimates, there are
eight million children under six whose parents work, and
fewer than one million slots available in licensed child care
centers to accommodate them.[2] Even primary grade children
of working mothers may require before and after school care.

---

[1]"...five aspects of the child's personality: the physi-
cal, emotional, social, creative, and cognitive selves." Joann
Hendrick. Total Learning for the Whole Child. St. Louis, MO:
C.V. Mosby Company, 1980, p. 9.

[2]Dennis Meredith, "Day Care: The Nine-to-Five Dilemma,"
Psychology Today, February 1986, pp. 36-44.

The quality day care program is designed to meet a variety of children's needs while addressing the concerns of their parents. Children's needs are physical, cognitive, and psychosocial in nature and are manifested in a wide variety of ways. To some extent, development occurs according to a prespecified sequence and is, therefore, predictable in nature. On the other hand, the past 25 years of research into early development have highlighted the individuality and uniqueness of each child's growth and learning. Above all, we realize that children must be interacted with in ways that affirm, rather than deny, their exceptionality.

It is the components, or special features of the program, which speak to the needs of the child, family, and even the staff. These must be designed, implemented, and modified in a fashion that promotes the overall development of every youngster, while at the same time cultivating the child's relationship with the family. Staff, too, have growth and esteem needs that must be addressed by program components. Response to these often determines overall program effectiveness.

The components of a day care program are dependent upon a number of factors. Influences include the source of program funding, the goals of affiliate agencies, the location of the program, the clients served, and the training and experience of the caregiving and support staff. For example, programs receiving federal funds often require that some sort of food be provided when young children receive care for more than a few hours per day.

Extensive health care provisions are often found in those day care programs sponsored by hospitals. The components of urban programs may vary significantly from those of rural areas, and the income level of families served can also affect the number and extent of the features of a day care center. Staff experience and training are factors because various approaches to teacher education and different models of early childhood education emphasize contrasting aspects of child development and methods of facilitating these.

Identification and development of appropriate components for day care programs require careful consideration of legal and funding source requirements, staff capabilities, and child and family needs. Components should not be devised at random but must be strongly tied to the philosophy and goal statements of the program. Planning the uses of personnel and supplies needed to implement a day care program is crucial. Seeking feedback from those who will participate in or be affected by a component should be done during the developmental stage rather than at the point of implementation.

While components of day care programs can vary greatly from one center to another, certain elements are basic to all programs concerned with the care and education of young children. The first of these is <u>custodial care</u>. While the isolation of a custodial care component is not obvious in high-quality settings, it is important to discuss it in order to stress the significance of the caregiver's response to a child's needs for warmth, dry clothing, food, sleep, and exercise. These services should not be delivered without individualized interaction and warmth; the absence of custodial care, even when a program addresses other needs of the child, can be a serious detriment to overall development. This was pointed out years ago by the government studies that examined the value of a nutritious breakfast on the readiness of children for learning. In addition, the physical needs of young children are paramount in their lives. They have not yet learned to defer the urge to rest, eat, or eliminate. Refusal by the caregiver to respond to these demands can render a youngster incapable of other participation in the program.

A second cardinal component of day care programs includes the environment, curriculum, materials, equipment,
and techniques utilized by teachers: the _education_ component. Although approaches to childhood education vary
widely, the objectives and types of materials utilized are
often similar. Frequently, for example, caregivers focus on
building the social, cognitive, sensorial, and communication
skills of youngsters.[3] Also common are materials and equipment designed to promote creativity, self-esteem, independence, and mutual respect.[4] Many day care centers provide
interest areas for art, music, block, and dramatic play,
looking at books, sand and water play, and woodworking.

Outdoor as well as indoor activities are an important
part of the educational component. If some day care providers think of outdoor experiences primarily as opportunities to facilitate muscle skills and coordination, many
others are familiar with the use of nature to promote cognitive and social growth.

The educational component also consists of the milieu
in which child and adult learning occurs. The atmosphere

---

[3]Sarah Hammond Leeper, et al. _Good Schools for Young
Children: A Guide for Working with Three- Four- and Five-
Year-Old Children_, Fifth Edition. New York: Macmillan Pub-
lishing Company, 1984.

[4]Alice S. Honig and J. Ronald Lally. _Infant Caregiving:
A Design for Training_. Syracuse, NY: Syracuse University
Press, 1981.

created by human response to people and situations, by room arrangement, by amount of light, heat and quality of air can either promote or hinder learning.

Many day care and other early childhood programs utilize an integrated approach to the curriculum where the educational component is concerned. Curriculum areas are not taught separately as math, science, or language arts lessons. Rather information is presented in a correlated fashion, in which it is believed that many young children learn best.[5] The preschool-age youngster is not capable of comprehending the separation of learning into compact bits of information or skills as is often expected in the elementary school. Therefore, the planning of the curriculum content, the selection of equipment and materials, and the choice of teaching methods to be employed by staff must be thorough. Those involved in curriculum implementation must also alert parents to the objectives of the educational component if there is to be content and skills carryover to the home. In addition, regular assessment of children's development and learning should be undertaken to determine the rate of achievement of the objectives.

The environment of a day care center is as important as any other element. While it is being treated as a part of the education component it regularly affects both children

---

[5]Sarah Hammond Leeper et al., Good Schools for Young Children: A Guide for Working with Three- Four- and Five-Year-Old Children, Fifth Edition. New York: Macmillan Publishing Company, 1984, p. 3.

and adults. Environment has aspects both visible and invisible to program participants. For example, the layout of children's and adults' spaces should be attractive and easy to function in. There should be a sense of spaciousness, not clutter. In classrooms, materials should be accessible to children and equipment child-size. The arrangement of the room should be one inviting youngsters to move freely without interfering with the activities of others. There should be spaces for active and quiet, group and individual activities. Adults, too, need places to call their own, for planning or a quiet time.

Environment is also an invisible factor that is, nonetheless felt by everyone. A room's temperature and lighting affect people making them feel comfortable or uncomfortable in their setting. Part of this aspect of environment, which we will call "atmosphere," is comprised of the interactions that occur in a center. When individuals are caring and cooperative with one another, the atmosphere conveys warmth and comfort. When that warmth is lacking both adults and children may feel ill at ease and the environment may be chaotic and unpleasant.

Environment, like all of the aspects of the day care program requires planning, regular evaluation, and modification. Even when adults are caring and plan extensively for children an inappropriate environment can prevent a program from functioning effectively (see "Evaluation" bibliography).

A third vital component of day care programs deals with the _health and safety_ of children, parents, and staff. Neither children or adults can function purposefully in a setting where they fear for their safety. For this reason, the environment must be free of debris, rodents, insects, and other factors which create a sense of discomfort. Parents should not be afraid to come to the center nor should they worry that their children are in danger of accident, injury, or subject to child molesters in their absence. Mothers and fathers should not have to worry that unsanitary conditions or inadequate supervision by staff will result in their youngster's illness. These fears are especially real at a time when parents have heard so much about the AIDS epidemic and the day care health problems which have received wide publicity.[6]

Staff members should not have to fear for their safety if they must be first to open the building or last to leave it. Caregivers should be assured of adequate support and coverage in every classroom, even when others are absent due to illness or vacation. A conscientious director also bears in mind that the daily stresses of working with children affect the mental health of child care workers.

---

[6]Marian Blum, "The Day Care Cloaca," _The Day Care Dilemma: Women and Children First_. Lexington, MA: Lexington Books, 1983, pp. 67-76.

For the parents of all young children, especially infants and toddlers, the decision to place a child in day care can be very traumatic. So traumatic, that it may interfere with their ability to function productively at work. Sensitivity on the part of the caregivers to the emotional needs of parents is one way to support the parent-child relationship as well as the mental health of both parties.

Some of the health needs of children correspond directly to those addressed by the custodial care component. The need to eat, rest, exercise, and eliminate regularly is critical to all humans. Changes in behavior may also be indicators of poor health. As a child health advocate, the day care provider must become attuned to signals of illness from a child. Isolation areas must be provided for children who are ill in order to protect the others.

In many states handicapped children were granted access to day care programs which receive federal funds by Public Law 94-142. In such cases the staff of a center becomes involved in child health in unique ways. Caregivers may serve as members of interdisciplinary teams that develop individualized educational programs (I.E.P.) for children with special needs. These day care providers work closely with physicians, psychologists, therapists, and transportation personnel. The teacher also assumes responsibility for watching the day-to-day progress of the child and steps made toward the achievement of the objectives specified by the I.E.P.

An essential aspect of the health and safety component is the obligation of the staff to provide more than a safe and healthy environment. Workers must also be health and safety educators. Even in infancy, children can begin to learn the basics of good nutrition and to learn which situations, people, and objects may be dangerous to them. Therefore, this component includes carefully planned activities to promote health and safety education.

The social services component may take one of several different forms in the day care setting. In its simplest style, this component may be a file of resources for assistance with financial, housing, food, energy, or other family needs. At a more sophisticated level, a center has its own social worker who acts as a mediator between the family and other social agencies to negotiate and assist with completion of necessary paperwork. In instances of spouse, child, drug, or alcohol abuse, or other family crisis, a social services component can mean the difference in a family's survival.

The fifth and final component to be discussed here[7] is that one devoted to staff development. The professional growth of staff may, quite literally, be the hinge upon which the overall success of a program swings. Staff development involves not only personnel training and continuing education but, more importantly, the growing recognition that each person brings individual expertise and value to the program. Avenues for professional development must continually be provided for all members of the day care staff. Offering occasional inservice programs does not meet the requirement of quality staff development.

Both direct service and support personnel need opportunities to attend workshops and conferences; participate in the activities of professional organizations; have access to literature in the field; visit agencies and programs providing similar services; and undertake special interest projects. The greatest benefit of such chances is their overall impact on the day care program. Staff who are consistently introduced to new information and skills are likely to practice what they have learned. A steady growth of new competencies is both reassuring and motivating. While caregivers need to

---

[7]Two other components, the administrative and parent involvement elements, are discussed elsewhere in this volume.

be told they are doing a good job, they must also be able to clearly see the results of their efforts. When children show developmental progress and new ability to perform tasks; when parents express pleasure with the program's impact on their child and are regularly involved at the center; when board and community members speak of the program's fine reputation, then staff are privy to the sort of job satisfaction that does not necessarily come from positive job evaluations or even from raises in salary. Caregivers and support staff who feel successful and rewarded by their work are more likely to make a personal commitment to working for a quality program, are less likely to be frequently absent from work, and are less likely to leave the program permanently.

As important as the planning and proper implementation of each component is, equally important is the process by which all components are interrelated. If components fail to function together smoothly, then all participants suffer. Day care directors are subject to many stresses, and a human response to those tensions may be to focus attention on those parts of the program that are most personally interesting and least pressure filled. As a result, some components, perhaps those most in need of attention, can suffer.

All program components require time for planning, evaluation, and modification. One way to assure equal attention
for every component is for the director to delegate authority
to those staff who have special interest in the activities
of each area. Caregiving and support personnel can undertake
the supervision of many home-school activities, edit the
center newsletter, coordinate staff training, or plan fund-
raising events. Parents can be valuable, assistants in carry-
ing out activities associated with various components.
Directors can also enlist the aid of board members and other
resource persons, thereby leaving the program's administrator
free to oversee each component and assess its success.

The real value of the compartmentalized day care program
is that each aspect speaks directly to some of the needs of
children, parents, staff, or community. The quality day
care/child development center stands out among children's
programs as one which demonstrates its awareness of participant needs on a continuing basis. Brazelton states,
"...ideal day care would make the parents' needs just as important as the children's... (it) then become(s) a kind of
extended family...."[8] The authors would add that the

----

[8]T. Berry Brazelton. Working and Caring. Reading, MA:
Addison-Wesley Publishing Company, 1985, p. 65.

administration and staff of day care programs have many of
the same support needs that can often be effectively met
through quality program components.

BIBLIOGRAPHY

Baranoff, Timy. <u>Kindergarten Minute by Minute</u>. Belmont, CA: Fearon Pitman Publishers, Inc., 1979.

    An overview of the kindergarten program from setup of the classroom to classroom management. This volume includes equipment lists and dozens of activity ideas that could easily be employed by caregivers working in school-age child care programs.

Brophy, Jeri E., Thomas L. Good, and Shari E. Nedler. <u>Teaching in the Preschool</u>. New York: Harper and Row Publishers, Inc., 1975.

    Procedures for assessing the developmental levels of young children, prescriptive teaching, scheduling activities, motivating and individualizing for children.

Brown, Janet (Ed.). <u>Curriculum Planning for Young Children</u>. Washington, DC: National Association for the Education of Young Children, 1982.

    Looks at curriculum from a concept and skills development standpoint. Sections are included on play, communication, exploration, and the arts. Implementation techniques are also covered.

Carlyon, Marsha, et al. <u>Early Childhood Teacher's Activities Handbook: A Resource Recipe for Early Childhood Learning Programs</u>. Englewood Cliffs, NJ: Prentice-Hall, Inc., 1981.

    Using a recipes for learning approach, this book throws together both teaching and program administration information. It provides forms for program management, lists of materials and equipment, and dozens of ideas for child development activities.

Chenfeld, Mimi Brodsky. <u>Creative Activities for Young Children</u>. New York: Harcourt Brace Jovanovich, 1983.

A valuable resource for teachers of young children emphasizing the input of the individual personality and philosophy of the teacher into curriculum planning and implementation. Sections are devoted to children's getting to know and understand their uniqueness, feelings, families and friends, colors, shapes, and numbers.

Cook, Ruth E., and Virginia B. Armbruster. Adapting Early Childhood Curricula.

Designed as an aid for those developing a curriculum for mainstreamed preschoolers. Techniques for analyzing individual learning styles and identifying appropriate teaching strategies. Symptoms of specific problems and disorders are provided.

Cozden, Courtney B. (Ed.). Language in Early Childhood Education. Washington, DC: National Association for the Education of Young Children, 1981.

Describes programs to develop the language of young children in day care and preschool settings. Differences in language growth at home and at school are discussed.

Croft, Doreen J. and Robert D. Hess. An Activities Handbook Teachers of Young Children. Boston, MA: Houghton Mifflin, 1985.

Activities, materials, equipment to enrich the day care program. A variety of concept areas are included and extensive bibliographies are provided. Arts, language, mathematics, ecology, science, and cooking are among the curriculum areas covered.

Cruikshank, Douglas E., David L. Fitzgerald, and Linda R. Jensen. Young Children Learning Mathematics. Boston: Allyn and Bacon, Inc., 1980.

Focuses on the young child's development of mathematical concepts, such as number, numeral, space, and the growth of problem solving skills. Provides lesson ideas.

Day, Barbara. Early Childhood Education: Creative Learning Activities, Second Edition. New York: Macmillan Publishing Co., Inc., 1983.

Focuses on organization and use of the learning environment. Learning centers for blocks, creative dramatics, science, mathematics, and movement, as well as outdoor play are discussed. Many sample games and activities are provided. Includes extensive appendices of resource materials.

Day, Barbara D. and Kay N. Drake. Early Childhood Education: Curriculum Organization and Classroom Management. Alexandria, VA: Association for Supervision and Curriculum Development, 1983.

Presents various ways of looking at and organizing the curriculum and managing the classroom. A supplement to set of filmstrips by A.S.C.D.

Debelak, Marianne, Judith Herr, and Martha Jacobson. Creating Innovative Classroom Materials for Teaching Young Children. New York: Harcourt Brace Jovanovich, Inc., 1981.

An illustrated curriculum guide with step-by-step procedures for making materials and strategies for their use. Suggestions are made for obtaining materials, and a bibliography of books and films is provided.

Eliason, Claudia Fuhriman, and Loa Thomson Jenkins. A Practic Guide to Early Childhood Curriculum. St. Louis, MO: C.V. Mosby Company, 1977.

The focus of this volume is on curriculum to develop chil dren's concepts. Many of these are listed along with a wide variety of activities in areas such as size and seriation, animals, weight and balance, music, and language. Unit plans are included for each concept area.

Endres, Jeanette Brakhane, and Robert E. Rockwell. Food, Nutr tion, and the Young Child. St. Louis, MO: C.V. Mosby Company, 1980.

Nutritional needs of children from birth through age five Nutrition education and food service management as they pertai to supervisors and program administrators.

Fiarotta, Phyllis. Snips and Snails and Walnut Whales: Nature Crafts for Children. New York: Workman Publishing Company, 1975.

Designed for the school-age child, a wealth of nature activities utilizing flowers, leaves, pine cones, sand and other things found outdoors. Crafts activities are easily arranged and inexpensive experiences for school-age child care.

Frost, Joe L. and Joan B. Kissinger. The Young Child and the Educative Process. New York: Holt, Rinehart and Winston, 1976.

Presents the historic and contemporary influences on early childhood education, provides an overview of child development, and suggests developing environments and activities to facilitate child growth. The appendices include a sample developmental checklist and information on commonly used standardized tests for screening young children.

Haas, Carolyn Buhai. Look at Me: Activities for Infants and Toddlers. Glencoe, IL: CBH Publishing, 1985.

Includes toys to make, movement games, and many other "recipes for learning." Haas clearly establishes that social-emotional development is the most important goal of play in the early years. Activities can be implemented using accessible materials.

Harlan, Jean. Science Experiences for the Early Childhood Years, Third Edition. Columbus, OH: Charles E. Merrill Publishing Company, 1984.

Discussion of science concepts and many lessons and activities on various science themes. Suggestions for materials and equipment are provided.

Hatoff, Sydelle, Claudia A. Byram, and Marion C. Hyson. Teacher's Practical Guide for Educating Young Children: A Growing Program. Boston: Allyn and Bacon, Inc., 1981.

Designed to assist the curriculum developer with the process of developing philosophy and goals and preparing space. Looks at observation and record keeping as tools for individualizing curriculum. Provides forms and work sheets useful in the program planning stages or when problem solving or promoting change.

Hendrick, Joanne. Total Learning: For the Whole Child. St. Louis, MO: C.V. Mosby Company, 1980.

Emphasizes the development of competence as a goal of curriculum. Explores factors that affect the curriculum, such as funding, grouping of children, and the program's educational philosophy. Children's physical, social, and cognitive growth is considered as essential outcome of effective curriculum.

Holt, Bess-Gene. Science with Young Children. Washington, DC: National Association for the Education of Young Children, 1977.

Focuses on the unique abilities and interests of the child as a science student. Describes the roles of the teacher as facilitator of learning and preparer of the environment.

Kamii, Constance. Number: In Preschool and Kindergarten. Washington, DC: National Association for the Education of Young Children, 1982.

A Piagetian-based introduction to numbers. Discusses use of preschool learning situations to teach the value of numbers to young children.

Langenbach, Michael and Teanna West Neskora. Day Care Considerations. Columbus, OH: Charles E., Merrill Publishing Company, 1977.

A broad look at many of the factors affecting day care programming from the viewpoint of the curriculum developer. A rationale for day care, samples of philosophy statements, and sample goals and objectives are provided. Theories of child development by outstanding spokespersons in the field are presented. Examples of curriculum applications for infancy through school-age are provided.

Leeper, Sarah Hammond, Ralph L. Witherspoon, and Barbara Day. Good Schools for Young Children, Fifth Edition. New York: Macmillan Publishing Company, 1984.

Designed to provide an overview of the characteristics of high quality preschool programs. Describes aspects of curriculum and other components of early childhood programs, such as environment, staffing, parent involvement, and working with the exceptional child.

Margolin, Edythe. Teaching Young Children at School and Home. New York: Macmillan, 1982.

Designed as a guide to both the educator and parent, this volume provides many suggestions for activities for working with the young child.

Marotz, Lynn, Jeanettia Rush, and Marie Cross. Health, Safety and Nutrition for the Young Child. Albany, NY: Delmar Publishers, Inc., 1985.

Addresses health and safety needs of children in early childhood settings. Includes focus on basic nutrition concepts and nutrition education. Useful as a guide or text for caregivers and parents. Excellent use of charts to describe childhood diseases and other health issues.

McCarthy, Melodie A., and John P. Houston. <u>Fundamentals of Early Childhood Education</u>. Cambridge, MA: Winthrop Publishers, Inc., 1980.

The basics of early childhood programs are covered in this volume. Emphasis is placed upon important development and learning theories. Issues in programming and curriculum development are presented along with the unique concerns of early childhood educators.

McElderry, Joanne S., and Linda E. Escobedo. <u>Tools for Learning: Activities for Young Children with Special Needs</u>. Denver, CO: Love Publishing, 1979.

Presents materials, techniques, and activities for the learning disabled or handicapped child.

Mitchell, Grace L., and Harriet Chmela. <u>I Am! I Can! The Daycare Handbook</u>. Stamford, CT: Greylock Publishers, 1977.

An extensive discussion of the world of day care. Provides techniques and procedures for admission of children to programs. The volume features a developmentally sequential curriculum.

Moore, G. et al. <u>Planning and Design Guidelines: Childcare Centers and Outdoor Play Environments</u>. Milwaukee, WI: Center for Architecture and Urban Planning Research, University of Wisconsin, 1979.

From the architect's viewpoint, ideas for the design of indoor and outdoor day care spaces. Practical for building from scratch or redesigning existing areas.

Morrison, George S. <u>Early Childhood Education Today</u>, Third Edition. Columbus, OH: Charles E. Merrill Publishing Company, 1984.

An excellent overview of the field. Chapters address the major theories and spokespersons in the field, day care, Head Start, Piaget, Montessori, and other critical topics. A popular textbook for preservice teachers exploring the history of and trends in early childhood education.

Newman, Dana. <u>The Early Childhood Teacher's Almanack: Activities for Every Month of the Year</u>. West Nyack, NY: Center for Applied Research in Education, Inc., 1984.

Presents a seasonal, almanack approach to curriculum for young children. Emphasis on holiday celebrations, the world of nature, recipes, arts and crafts projects for year around. Also introduces holidays from various cultures and religions.

<u>Nutrition Education for Preschoolers: A Resource Guide for
    Use in the Child Care Food Program</u>. Washington, DC:
    Superintendent of Documents, U.S. Government Printing
    Office, 1983.

    Instructional guides for nutrition education of children
and caregivers in day care settings. Audiovisuals and other
aids and teaching activities are listed.

Reinisch, Edith H., and Ralph E. Mincar, Jr. <u>Health of the
    Preschool Child</u>. New York: John Wiley and Sons, 1978.

    Describes the roles of child care providers in relation
to child health. Use of health observations, care of the ill
child, accident prevention, and provision of nutrition component are discussed.

Rich, Dorothy. <u>The Kids' After School Activity Book</u>. Bel-
    mont, CA: David S. Lake Publishers, 1985.

    For use at home or in school-age child care programs, a
book of activities for children ages eight to 12 years.
Activities include make-it projects, places to go, things to
see.

Robinson, Nancy M., et al. <u>A World of Children: Day Care and
    Preschool Institutions</u>. Monterey, CA: Brooks/Cole Pub-
    lishing Company, 1979.

    Presents a discussion of the role of child care as a re-
sponse to changes in American family life. Child care alternatives and the goals of various programs are described, along
with four national care models. Issues in care are presented
along with conclusions and recommendations for the future.

Saunders, R., and A. M. Bingham-Newman. <u>Piagetian Perspective
    for Preschools: A Thinking Book for Teachers</u>. Engle-
    wood Cliffs, NJ: Prentice-Hall, 1984.

    A guide for the early childhood educator who wants to
both comprehend basic Piagetian theory and incorporate it
into the classroom. Activities and techniques are included.

Seefeldt, Carol. <u>A Curriculum for Child Care Centers</u>.
    Columbus, OH: Charles E. Merrill Publishing Company,
    1974.

    A five part discussion of the foundation and components
of the child care curriculum. An overview of child care in
the United States, the people involved in programs, and the
play of young children are examined. A variety of curriculum
areas are discussed.

Seefeldt, Carol. <u>A Curriculum for Preschools</u>, Second Edition. Columbus, OH: Charles E. Merrill Publishing Company, 1980.

Sections of this guide to developing curriculum are devoted to the impact of human interaction on the program, children, parents, staff, and community; the importance of play; and the health of the child. Language, science, mathematics, social studies, and artistic experiences are among the areas of the curriculum covered.

Seefeldt, Carol. <u>Social Studies for the Preschool-Primary Child</u>, Second Edition. Columbus, OH: Charles E. Merrill Publishing Company, 1984.

This volume covers planning and implementing social studies curriculum for young children. An overview of concepts in the areas of history, geography, economics, and international education. Also discusses values classification as a component of curriculum.

Segal, Marilyn, and Abbey Manburg, (Eds.). <u>All About Child Care</u>. Fort Lauderdale, FL: Nova University, 1981.

Describes many of the kinds of programs available for young children. Discusses the needs of children and environment and curriculum to address these.

Taylor, Barbara J. <u>A Child Goes Forth</u>, Fifth Edition, Revised. Provo, UT: Brigham Young University Press, 1980.

A guide to planning the preschool curriculum. Includes exercises especially for parents and activities for teachers to conduct. Suggested teaching aides are listed and extensive bibliographies included.

Wanamaker, Nancy et al. <u>More Than Graham Crackers: Nutrition Education and Food Preparation with Young Children</u>. Washington, DC: National Association for the Education of Young Children, 1979.

Provides activities designed to familiarize young children with the nutritional benefits of foods from the four basic food groups.

<u>What to Do to Stop Disease in Child Day Care Centers: A Kit for Child Day Care Directors</u>. Washington, DC: Superintendent of Documents, U.S. Government Printing Office, 1985.

Contains handbooks on disease prevention and a handbook on contagious disease for directors, caregivers, parents. Three posters for health education are included.

Zigler, Edward, and Susan Muenchow, "Infectious Diseases in Day Care: Parallels Between Psychologically and Physically Healthy Care," <u>Review of Infectious Disease</u>, Vol. 8, No. 4, July-August 1986, pp. 514-520.

Reviews the effects of day care practices on child health. Examines the relationship between care which is psychologically healthy and diminished risk of infectious disease. Looks also at other factors impacting on child health in the day care setting, such as group size, staff-child ratios, and staff training.

WORKING WITH PARENTS AND COMMUNITY MEMBERS

Beginning with interest in family involvement in the kindergarten and elementary school, much has been said and written about the importance of parent participation in childhood education.[1] In the early childhood profession, virtually every conference of any significance includes an address or workshop devoted to increasing levels of parent cooperation and support in programs for young children.

Encouraging parents to participate in center activities is a special problem in the day care setting. While many mothers, fathers, and other primary caregivers would like to be more involved with their youngsters' child care programs, many factors interfere with this desire. There is, first of all, the fact that these are, for the most part, parents employed outside the home. Time constraints alone are a significant barrier to participation but added to that are the stresses of balancing professional and parenting roles.[2] For many parents extra time is required to transport their child to and from the day care center. With meals to be

---

[1]Eugenia Hepworth Berger. Parents as Partners in Education: The School and Home Working Together. St. Louis, MO: C.V. Mosby Company, 1981, pp. 47-70.

[2]Eloise Salholz, et al., "Feminism's Identity Crisis," Newsweek, March 31, 1986, pp. 58-59.

prepared, laundry and housework to be done, and errands to be run, little time is left over for other things.

Parent involvement is also affected by a variety of individual and family life concerns. Many mothers and fathers worry a great deal about the things missed during the long hours away from their children. They are concerned that lost time can never be made up and wonder about the long-term impact on the family.[3] Although research indicates this concern is probably unnecessary, it is certainly an understandable fear. Some parents cope with their apprehensions by detaching themselves from the child's day care day. They may feel powerless to understand or be part of what occurs during those hours, so it is easier to remain uninvolved.

A second factor of parent involvement in day care is rarely discussed. It is one that may be especially problematic in infant-toddler programs. This factor concerns competition between caregivers and parents for the attention of the child. Brazelton has written,

> All adults who care about babies are competitive with all other adults, and each would like to be the primary caretaker of the attractive helpless infant. Unconsciously we devalue the role of parents

---

[3]Deborah Fallows, "My Turn: What Day Care Can't Do," Newsweek, January 10, 1983, p. 8.

> to fulfill our own role as the important caretaker....[4]

Child care workers in the day care setting must be nurturers of the parent-child relationship, and allow mothers and fathers the opportunity to discover their youngster on their own. Although care providers may have expertise on child development in general, it is the parent who is generally the authority on his or her own child. Some caregivers inadvertently rob parents of this role by stressing the value of their interaction with the child and the use of academic jargon in the day care environment. Mothers and fathers may then pull away from involvement with the staff or the program.

Parent participation in the day care milieu can also be influenced by the past school experiences of mothers and fathers. If parents had feelings of low self-esteem as students or unhappy interactions with teachers or school administrators, they may feel uncomfortable at the day care center. This discomfiture is sometimes misinterpreted by staff as disinterest.

Cultural differences are sometimes responsible for lack of parent involvement in the day care setting. While some

---

[4]T. Berry Brazelton, in Marshall H. Klaus and John H. Kennell, <u>Parent-Infant Bonding</u>, Second Edition. St. Louis, MO: C.V. Mosby Company, 1982, p. 97.

Americans are comfortable with professionals at all levels, others may treat teachers with great deference. In such cases, parent-caregiver communication may be stilted.

Another cultural factor concerns the way in which family problems are dealt with. If parents feel that at-home crises must be handled entirely within the family and never discussed with outsiders, then problems which interfere with the family's participation in the center's program and even seriously disrupt the child's life may remain hidden from the day care staff.

Some hindrances to parent participation come from within the center. Staff may believe that parents have little to contribute to the program. Parental presence may be seen as a nuisance. Teachers may fear criticism from parents of their teaching methods or handling of the children. Some caregivers may have had unpleasant experiences with parents that have colored their reactions to all other families, causing them to overlook all of the potential benefits of parent involvement. Staff who have these feelings need direction and opportunities for positive outcomes from their interactions with parents.

Many direct and indirect roles can be played by the members of a child's family. Direct roles may be classroom, bus, or field trip aides; office or kitchen aides; editors of the center newsletter; or equipment/facility maintainers. Indirect service roles include organizers, of home-school activities; collectors of materials for children's projects; bakers for fund-raising cake sales; or coordinators of the center telephone tree. These roles need not be played only by mothers and fathers. Older siblings, aunts, uncles, and grandparents can also be involved in the program in these ways.

In the early childhood community, many of the original cues about home-school relationships came from the elementary school, including a rather narrow view of what constitutes parent involvement. The goals of day care demand that the interactions of parents and staff be envisioned in new ways in keeping with the changing American family.

Parent education is yet another facet of family involvement. If day care is to promote the growth of parent-child relations, the staff must accept some responsibility for facilitating parental understanding of child development and behavior in a number of ways. Perhaps those most overlooked are the messages that come through parent-teacher and teacher-child interactions. Caregiving staff may overlook the impact of their modeling, including the range of responses to child communication and behaviors, on the way parents interact with their youngsters at home. When teachers support the growth of parenting skills, they work toward enhancing the awareness of mothers and fathers of their children. Rather than advancing their own expertise, these caregivers cultivate the knowledge and role of the parent.

Parent education is usually dealt with in a class or workshop aimed at providing certain information or instruction in basic parenting skills. The interests and needs of parents should always be assessed prior to the development of a parent education program rather than randomly selecting training topics. Careful planning with attention to the trainer, methods and materials, opportunities for parents' input, training environment, and methods of evaluation will promote the success of parenting education. Among the areas of special interest to mothers and fathers of young children are milestones in development, children's books and toys, and handling discipline problems.

Family members are not the only persons who can make a valuable contribution to the day care program. Many community members have skills and expertise that can benefit children, parents, and staff. These persons should be regularly and actively sought by parents and staff. Local colleges, businesses, service clubs and organizations can be sources of resource persons.

Local colleges can provide both student teachers and consultants. While accepting student teachers for practicum experiences is a great responsibility for a day care center administrator and staff, the center reaps many benefits. The enthusiasm and energy of the learner and the extra hands to assist with all of the children's activities are only two of the positive outcomes.

When assistance is needed in program development or staff training, the faculty of early childhood, child care, child development, or other departments can be of considerable assistance.[5] Their observations, input into training activities, and participation as members of the day care center policy board provide a considerable level of expertise that can positively affect the quality of the overall program.

The business community can also be a valuable asset to the child care program. The day care director can find helpful resources for funding, program development, and staff training among business leaders. Corporations have begun to directly address the child care needs of their employees through business-sponsored day care centers[6] (see "Issues" essay). The business community has begun to realize the

---

[5]Kathleen Pullan Watkins and Lucius Durant, Jr. The Early Childhood Director's Staff Development Handbook, Englewood Cliffs, NJ: Prentice-Hall, Inc., 1987.

[6]Andrea Fooner, "Who's Minding the Kids?," Working Women, May 1982, pp. 99-102.

benefits of the elimination of parental child care concerns. The door is now wide open for many new working arrangements between day care and the corporate world.

Senior citizens are another group of potential contributors to the child care center. Many children lack grandparent figures as a result of changes in family lifestyle. Grandparents and grandchildren do not always live in close proximity. Older adults may find themselves forced into retirement without chances to share their knowledge, skills, and life experience. Involvement in a day care/child development program can address both needs, those of the child and those of the older adult. There are a number of successful models of intergenerational programs upon which new programs may be based (see the bibliography).

One of the most important relationships to be cultivated by the day care staff is with the members of the policy board or community resource council. Even when not mandated by the law, community involvement should be sought by all center staff. Many educational program administrators forget that their programs have a place and role in the overall community. After a time, they begin to function in a fashion that negates the impact that day care has on the family and, ultimately, on society. When this breakdown in communications occurs, chances are lost for the staff and program to play the crucial advocacy roles for children and families. Furthermore, the community has lost its opportunity to provide feedback to the center.

Day care program administrators must regularly face legal, ethical, health, and financial issues. Careful selection of board members with the appropriate expertise provides both the forum for and information necessary to promote effective decision making. Inclusion of members of the business community, an attorney, a pediatrician, a member of the clergy, and a parent, as well as other resource persons creates a well-rounded board.

There are many useful techniques for involving parents and members of the community in the day care program. Parents' skills, interests, and availability should be pinpointed at the time a child is first enrolled. Talking about the need for parent involvement is by itself an inadequate method of promoting participation. Parents must be individually sought out for special projects and tasks, not once a year but frequently. Roles offered to families must be within their capabilities. If parents feel successful, they are more likely to continue to be involved. They should be recognized for their contribution, and the value of their time and input recognized.

While parents have some opportunities to learn about the program through their children and the staff, other methods must be utilized to involve community members. Staff can discuss the center's workings with their own families, friends, and neighbors. Articles about the program can be published in local newspapers, and a center newsletter can be distributed throughout the community. Invitations to "open house" can be sent to a wide range of persons who may be interested in involvement.

One of the more serious concerns of the early childhood profession is the great number of myths about day care that continue to flourish.[7] Many believe that day care is bad for children and endangers the family. Others believe that centers are hotbeds of disease and, as such, represent a danger to children. Still others are certain that some child care workers are actual or potential sex offenders and child abusers. Unless these misconceptions are clarified through the advocacy of persons in the field parents utilizing services, and members of the board it will continue to be difficult to achieve effective levels of community involvement.

The subject of community participation in day care cannot be addressed without mention of centers' vital links to other child and family service agencies. These should range from the feeder schools that accept children from day care into kindergarten or first grade programs, to the wide array of family crisis groups. The day care staff must investigate those programs in the community which respond to family needs,

---

[7]Marian Blum. The Day Care Dilemma: Women and Children First, Lexington, MA: Lexington Books, 1983.

exchanging information with them so that a mutual understanding of philosophy and goals exists. In addition to making information available to parents through the center's social services component, the importance of networking should not be overlooked.

The relationship of day care centers to the public school system is increasingly important. Many programs are located in school buildings, either because they are part of a school system or because space is allocated for child care through a rental arrangement. Unfortunately, the history of relationships between day care staff and elementary and secondary school staff is not always a positive one. Often this is due to misconceptions about attitudes and roles by both parties.

The most important reason for effective relationships is the exchange of information which enables teachers and caregivers to provide appropriate programs for children. Day care staff need to known how to better prepare children for the primary grades. Elementary teachers must be able to challenge and support youngsters with preschool experience (see "Issues" bibliography).

In the absence of abundant federal funds for human services, programs serving children and families must band together. United they can lobby for needed fiscal appropriations and legislation, avoid service duplication, and provide a better response to social and educational needs.

BIBLIOGRAPHY

Auerbach, Stevanne. Choosing Child Care: A Guide for
    Parents. New York: Dutton, 1981.

    Provides guidelines for parents who need to make choices
about day care for their children. Explores advantages of
babysitters, family day care homes, center-based care, and
programs to meet special needs. Suggests what parents should
look for during site visits and provides useful checklists.

Beers, Marley Clevenger, et al. Parent Involvement in Day
    Care: A Resource Manual for Day Care Providers. Wash-
    ington, DC: Creative Associates, Inc.

    Parent involvement is defined and benefits outlined.
Guidelines are provided for developing a parent participation
program, and 14 models of parent involvement from across the
country are described. Stresses importance of home-school
communication.

Beginnings: Multi-Age Caregiving, Vol. 2, No. 1, Spring 1985.

    An entire issue of Beginnings on multi-age caregiving,
including articles on intergenerational programs, volunteer
workers, and children as caregivers.

Berger, Eugenia H. Parents as Partners in Education. St.
    Louis, MO: C.V. Mosby Company, 1981.

    Includes an historic overview of family life and child-
rearing. Describes opportunities for parent involvement in
home and school-based programs. Attention is given to the
training and development of parents' leadership skills. Looks
at the factors which promote or inhibit parent involvement in
schools.

Bergstrom, Joan M., and Linda Joy. Going to Work? Choosing
    Care for Infants and Toddlers? A Parent's Guide. Wash-
    ington, DC: Day Care Council of America, 1981.

    Guidelines for parental assessment of child care environ-
ments and caregivers to enable selection of appropriate services. Looks at center-based and family day care.

Bigner, Jerry J. Parent-Child Relations: An Introduction to
    Parenting, Second Edition. New York: Macmillan Pub-
    lishing Company, 1985.

    A volume devoted in full to the development of the
parent-child relationship from infancy through early adult-
hood. Roles of parents and surrogate parents are discussed,
as is the impact of each stage of development on interactions
between adults and children.

Bonfield, Phyllis K. "Working Solutions for Working Parents,"
    Management World, Vol. 15, No. 2, February 1986, pp. 8-10.

    A discussion of the problems and stresses faced by work-
ing parents with young children. The "child care issue" con-
fronting the business and corporate worlds is explored.

Brazelton, T. Berry. "Issues for Working Parents," American
    Journal of Orthopsychiatry, Vol. 56, No. 1, January
    1986, pp. 14-25.

    Discusses the dangers to families of inadequate substi-
tute care for infants of working parents. Reviews issues
such as parental leave for arrival of new babies, and early
separation of parents and infant.

Brazelton, T. Berry. Working and Caring. Reading, MA:
    Addison-Wesley Publishing Company, Inc., 1985.

    Describes the problems common to working parents with
young children. Proposes pragmatic solutions. Discusses
parents' interactions with a variety of caregivers. Provides
a rationale for parents to remain at home with their newborn
during the first three months of life.

Brigham Young University Press (Eds.). How to Involve Parents
    in Early Childhood Education. Provo, UT: Brigham Young
    University Press, 1982.

    History of family involvement in early childhood pro-
grams, current status, and techniques for enhancing parent
participation in programs for young children.

Brock, Henry C. III. A Practical Guide: Parent Volunteer
    Programs in Early Childhood Education. Hamden, CT:
    Shoestring Press, 1976.

    Describes the planning and implementation processes of
parent involvement programs. Financial and legal implications
of parent participation in early childhood education are discussed. Sample forms are provided.

Bromwich, Rose M. Working with Parents and Infants: An Interactional Approach. Austin, TX: Pro-Ed, 1981.

Provides the rationale for the interactional approach to working with parents and babies. Describes research study conducted by the author, case studies, and outcomes of intervention approaches.

Clarke-Stewart, Alison. Child Care in the Family. New York: Academic Press, 1977.

Suggests alternatives to day care outside of the home for working parents. Shared care of young children by mothers and fathers, teen-age and senior "family-aides" are other examples of child care arranged within the home.

Cohen, Marlene Cresci, et al. The Intergenerational Caregiving Program: A Replication Manual. Arlington, VA: ERIC Document Reproduction Service, 1981.

Provides a rationale for intergenerational caregiving, suggestions for volunteer recruitment, training curriculum, and guidelines for volunteer supervision.

Dail, Paula W., "Who Will Mind the Child? A Dilemma for Many Employed Parents," Journal of Home Economics, Vol. 74, No. 1, Spring 1982, pp. 22-23.

Examines the impact of day care on child development and family. Presents research findings and responds to criticism that day care undermines family life.

Dreskin, William, and Wendy Dreskin. The Day Care Division: What's Best for You and Your Child. New York: M. Evans and Co., Inc., 1983.

Written by a couple who became concerned about the impact of day care on children while working as day care directors. Provides counterpoints for maternal doubts about engaging in full-time childrearing. Solutions to child care needs, such as job sharing, are discussed via case studies. A chapter is included on communicable illness in day care centers.

Endsley, R. C., and M. R. Bradbard. Quality Day Care: A Handbook of Choices for Parents and Caregivers. Englewood Cliffs, NJ: Prentice-Hall, 1981.

Provides a guide for parents and others attempting to identify appropriate day care facilities for children. Checklists for evaluating the day care environment are included.

Filstrup, Jane Merrill, and Dorothy W. Gross. <u>Monday through Friday: Day Care Alternatives</u>. New York: Teachers College Press, 1982.

Nine families describe how they solved their need for child care and balanced their child's and family needs. Care by househusband, relatives, a nanny, at a playgroup, via a babysitting cooperative, in a family day care home, and in a center are discussed.

Galinsky, Ellen. "How to Work with Working Parents," <u>Child Care Information Exchange</u>, June 1984, pp. 1-4.

Description of the many issues faced by parents of children in day care with emphasis on stresses experienced. Solutions are suggested to enable caregivers to communicate effectively with and support families.

Galinsky, Ellen. "How Understanding Parental Growth Will Help You as a Caregiver," <u>Child Care Information Exchange</u>, September 1980, pp. 25-32.

Looks at parental growth and its impact on the parent-child relationship as observed by child care providers. Suggests that caregivers both observe and attempt to understand parental development and also be attuned to their own influence on parent-child relationships.

Glickman, Beatrice Marden, and Nesher Bass Springer. <u>Who Cares for the Baby? Choices in Child Care</u>. New York: Schocken Books, 1979.

Designed to help parents assess available day care alternatives and make a selection based on the needs of their particular child. An appendix of day care referral agencies is provided.

Gordon, Thomas. <u>P.E.T.: Parent Effectiveness Training</u>. New York: New American Library, 1970.

Classic volume of techniques to improve parenting skills and maximize the effectiveness of parent-child communication. Factors inhibiting communication are described.

Honig, Alice S. <u>Parent Involvement in Early Childhood Education</u>. Washington, DC: National Association for the Education of Young Children, 1975.

The rights of parents in relation to childhood education, examples of parent involvement programs, and suggestions for evaluation of the success of parent participation in programs.

Horowitz, Ellen Gonchar, "Parent-Caregiver Communication in Two Kinds of Day Care Settings," Child Care Quarterly, Vol. 13, No. 2, Summer 1984, pp. 142-148.

A comparison of levels of parent-caregiver interaction in a neighborhood-based and employer-sponsored, on-site day care facility. Findings indicated low levels of communication at both sites and showed discrepancies in caregiver and parent interpretation of the frequency of discussion of family issues

"How to Choose a Good Early Childhood Program," Young Children, Vol. 39, No. 1, November 1983, p. 83.

Provides criteria to enable parents to assess the program, staff and environment in day care and preschool settings and select the best one for their child and family.

Joffe, Carole E. Friendly Intruders: Childcare Professionals and Family Life. Berkeley, CA: University of California Press, 1977.

Summarizes a research study designed to examine child care policy issues. Differences in the needs of black and white families where child care workers are involved. Concerned with the emergence of professionalism among early childhood educators.

Johnson, Sallie. Bridging Generations: A Handbook for Intergenerational Child Care. Soquel, CA: The Elvirita Lewis Foundation, 1980.

Suggestions for recruiting and orienting older people as staff in child care centers. Based on the existing Intergenerational Child Care Center sponsored by the Elvirita Lewis Foundation.

Klinman, Debra G., Rhiana Kohl, and The Fatherhood Project. Fatherhood U.S.A. New York: Garland Publishing, 1984.

A complete guide to programs, services, legal issues, and resources for and affecting American fathers. An excellent resource for anyone working with families.

Kurcher, Dan, "Finding the Best Day Care for Your Child," Better Homes and Gardens, June 1984, pp. 25-26, 32.

Describes child care alternatives and suggestions for parents to use when selecting a day care program.

Lamb, Michael E. (Ed.). Nontraditional Families: Parenting and Child Development. Hillsdale, NJ: Lawrence Erlbaum Associates, 1982.

A wide range of topics related to the growth and development of the child in the contemporary family are discussed. Examples include the day care environment, degrees of parental involvement in infant care, two-provider families, and others. Contributions by specialists in family and child development.

Levitan, Sar A., and Karen Cleary Alderman. Child Care and ABC's Too. Baltimore, MD: Johns Hopkins University Press, 1975.

Describes the characteristics of working mothers and the impact on the family of child care availability and services. Discusses different kinds of child care facilities available to parents, and provides a brief history of nursery-kindergarten education in the United States.

Manberg, Abbey, "Parent Involvement: A Look at Practices that Work," Child Care Information Exchange, January 1985, pp. 9-11.

"Tried and true" techniques for maximizing parent participation in early childhood programs.

Maynard, Fredelle. The Child Care Crisis: The Real Costs of Day Care for You -- and Your Child. Ontario, Canada: Penguin Books, 1985.

Draws the conclusion, based on research, family interviews, and opinions of specialists, that alternative child care for children under three can have a negative impact. Paints a vivid picture of the potential damage to child health and development from day care. Foreword by Burton White.

Miller, Bette L., and Ann L. Wilmhurst. Parents and Volunteers in the Classroom: A Handbook for Teachers. San Francisco: R and E Research Associates, 1975.

The complete guide to working with parents in schools. Planning, recruitment, orientation, and uses of volunteer workers are discussed. Amusing and interesting descriptions of various personality types and suggestions for working effectively with them are included. A parents' guide for working with children and volunteer activity cards are provided.

Mulford, Caroline. <u>Child Care and Nursing Home Residents:</u>
<u>Getting the Elderly Involved</u>. Washington, DC: National
Committee to Preserve Social Security and Medicare, 1984.

Description of the program at Children's Family Center,
Mechanicsburg, PA. Values to children and older adults of an
intergenerational care program.

Nedler, Shari E., and Oralie D. McAfee. <u>Working with Parents:</u>
<u>Guidelines for Early Childhood and Elementary Teachers</u>.
Belmont, CA: Wadsworth Publishing, 1979.

History of the roles of parents in schools and impact on
the present. Describes the processes for planning involvement
programs, including goal setting, strategies for involvement,
and parent education. Discusses model programs in early childhood centers and schools and the roles of parents as program
advisors and policy makers.

Rice, F. Philip. <u>A Working Mother's Guide to Child Develop-</u>
<u>ment</u>. Englewood Cliffs, NJ: Prentice-Hall, 1979.

Provides a supportive and informative guide to child
development, child-care alternatives, and family needs.
Offers working women encouragement with belief that the
quality of parenting is more important than the quantity of
time spent.

Rockwell, Robert E., and James M. Comer. <u>School Volunteer</u>
<u>Program: A Manual for Coordinators</u>. Athens, Ohio:
Midwest Teacher Corps Network, Ohio University, 1978.

Describes practical aspects of developing and operating
a school volunteer program.

Rothenberg, B. Anne. <u>Parentmaking: A Practical Handbook for</u>
<u>Teaching Parent Classes About Babies and Toddlers</u>. Menlo
Park, CA: Banster Press, 1982.

Guide to teaching classes for parents on child rearing
skills. Includes goals for teaching, sample lectures, hand-
outs, and teaching techniques suggestions. Useful for those
involved in developing and implementing parent education programs.

Rutherford, Robert B., Jr., and Eugene Edgar. <u>Teachers and</u>
<u>Parents: A Guide to Interaction and Cooperation</u>. Bos-
ton: Allyn and Bacon, Inc., 1979.

Offers problem solving techniques for use by teachers working with parents of young children. Suggests need to promote goals, information, and values sharing by both parties.

Scarr, Sandra. <u>Mother Care/Other Care</u>. New York: Basic Books, 1984.

Discusses the various problems faced by working mothers and the needs of their children. The importance of the mother-child relationship is described although Scarr stresses that others can provide valuable input into the child's early life. Child care options are explored.

Seefeldt, Carol, et al. <u>Young and Old Together: A Training Manual for Intergenerational Programs</u>. Arlington, VA: ERIC Document Reproduction Service, 1979.

Training curriculum and strategies for older volunteer workers in child care settings.

Siegel-Gorelick. <u>The Working Parents' Guide to Child Care: How to Find the Best Care for Your Child</u>. Boston: Little, Brown and Company, 1983.

Provides an overview to the many personal and practical considerations that go into selection of child care by parents. Assessing day care personnel and environments is discussed, as well as the signs that might indicate that a parent needs to change the caregiving arrangements.

Smith, Teresa. <u>Parents and Preschool</u>, Vol. 6, Oxford Pre-school Research Project, Ypsilanti, MI: High/Scope Press, 1980.

Reports on one component of the research project conducted in Britain by Jerome Bruner and colleagues. Describes policies of various programs regarding parent involvement. Compares levels of parent participation in different programs.

Stark, Giovanna. <u>There Is a Choice: Choosing Good Infant and Child Day Care</u>, Final Report and Executive Summary. Washington, DC: U.S. Department of Health and Human Services, March 1984.

Report of a one-year project to educate consumers about the components and characteristics of high-quality day care. This project was completed in urban, rural-migrant, and suburban areas in California. Parameters included inservice education for health care practitioners, videocassette presentations for parents, printed information for consumers and educators, and group meetings.

Sung, Keju-taik, "The Role of Day Care for Teenage Mothers in Public School," Child Care Quarterly. Vol. 10, No. 2, Summer 1981, pp. 113-124.

Describes a day care program for teen mothers on-site at a public school, and its role in encouraging young parents to complete their education.

Taylor, Katherine W. Parents and Children Learn Together, Third Edition. New York: Teachers College Press, 1981.

The role of parent cooperative programs in supporting the needs of young families. Organizing a parent cooperative center to provide childhood and parenting education is discussed. Emphasis is placed on the learning needs of parents.

Texas Department of Human Resources. Day Care, Families, and Stress. Austin, TX: Texas Dept. of Human Resources.

Explores the causes of stress that are experienced by children, families, and caregivers participating in center-based and family day care. Discusses changes that can reduce stress levels for all.

Tizard, B., J. Mortimore, and B. Burchell. Involving Parents in Nursery and Infant Schools: A Source Book for Teachers. London: Grant McIntyre, 1981.

Designed to present an alternative approach to viewing parent involvement in the preschool setting. Reports on a research project conducted in England, although the issues raised are similar to those concerns of American early childhood educators. Shows empathy for the needs of both parents and teachers.

White, Burton L., "Viewpoint: Should You Stay Home with Your Baby?," Young Children, Vol. 37, No. 1, November 1981, pp. 11-17.

Proposes that parent or family care is generally preferable to other forms of child care. Suggests those instances where alternative care is acceptable.

Wilson, Marlene. <u>Effective Management of Volunteer Programs</u>.
St. Paul, MN: Volunteer Management Associates, 1976.

Recruitment, task delegation, evaluation of volunteer
services. Management and leadership theories also described.

Winston, Pamela J., Ann P. Turnbull, and Jan Blacher. <u>Select-</u>
<u>ing a Preschool: A Guide for Parents of Handicapped</u>
<u>Children</u>. Austin, TX: Pro-Ed, 1984.

Guidelines to enable parents to make an informed choice
regarding day care or preschool programs for their handicapped youngster. Considers staff, facilities, curriculum,
and other components of the program. Legal rights of parents
and children, according to P.L. 94-142 are described.

EVALUATING DAY CARE PROGRAMS

> Evaluation is implied in the very process
> of (program) planning, for it is the act
> of placing a value on something, of deter-
> mining its merit.[1]

Although many day care centers periodically look at children's progress and may also rate staff performance, there
is little effort to systematically study the effects of child
care on participants, both child and adult. When assessment
is built into the program and conducted regularly, opportunities are created to modify components as required and prevent minor difficulties or inconsistencies from escalating
and becoming serious problems.

One of the problems that appears to interfere with regular evaluation of the day care setting is attitudinal. Many
early childhood educators mistakenly believe that the process
of assessing programmatic outcomes is complicated and time-
taking. Evaluation is linked with the use of procedures for
statistical analysis, another intimidator.

Another reason that many administrators shy away from
studying program outcomes is the fear that the results of

---

[1]J. Galen Saylor, et al. <u>Curriculum Planning: For
Teaching and Learning</u>, Fourth Edition. New York: Holt,
Rinehart and Winston, 1981, p. 316.

evaluation may reflect negatively on the director. A stigma is attached to all forms of educational evaluation which suggests that the purpose of assessment is to determine what is being done incorrectly. Evaluation may not be seen as another of the tools for improving program quality but as a threat to the center's leadership.

Day care administrators may also become caught up in the concrete aspects of the program. How the facility looks; the observable interactions of children, parents, and teachers; the day-to-day activities planned by teachers and conducted with children may all seem more important than a rating scale, checklist, or other written tool for evaluation. A director may trust that those and other observable behaviors of program participants are by themselves adequate indications that all is functioning properly. The difficulty with this assumption is that it is a subjective one. It denies the very real possibility that the day care administrator does not see or broadly interpret all of the activities of the program.

Evaluation tools and procedures provide the criteria through which a more objective view of the day care program can be taken. This is possible because appropriately developed, evaluation is never random. Instead it is a carefully designed system to provide feedback on all aspects of the program. Each element of the assessment process should ask specific questions about the facets of programs it studies, such as: "Given the stated purposes of this component (goals and objectives), what activities have been successfully conducted in order to reach these ends?" Each evaluation item is another of the criteria for achieving overall progress.

Curriculum evaluation spokesperson Michael Scriven has written about two types of evaluation.[2] Formative methods are concerned with smaller pieces of a program that yield immediate results and make quick modifications possible. Summative methods look at broader elements of the program and attainment of long-term goals. This form of assessment examines the overall outcomes of the program.

Examples of these two types of evaluation include assessment of the outcomes of staff training (the formative method) and annual developmental screening to determine degrees of children's progress (an example of summative evaluation).

A number of evaluation models have been developed over the years. One of these is based upon principles developed by Ralph Tyler in the 1930s.[3] Called the "father of

---

[2]Michael Scriven, "The Methodology of Evaluation," In Robert E. Stake (Ed.). Perspective on Curriculum Evaluation. Chicago, IL: Rand McNally and Company, 1967, pp. 40-43.

[3]Ralph W. Tyler. Basic Principles of Curriculum and Instruction. Chicago, IL: University of Chicago Press, 1950.

behavioral objectives," Tyler uses pre-determined objectives to measure changes in the behavior of program participants. The behavioral objectives model is primarily summative in nature, relying on the products of the program to measure outcomes. This model is one way to evaluate the impact of day care. The uses of objectives for education has been stressed for some time in elementary and secondary schooling. Early childhood educators have taken a rather negative view of these because of their affiliation with non-humanist philosophy. Behavioral objectives have been seen as a form of engineering children's thinking, but this may be too narrow a conception of their purpose to be realistic.

Every day teachers and caregivers in day care settings provide a variety of types of reinforcement for those behaviors deemed appropriate for children. The use of behavioral objectives is simply a way of pre-specifying these as well as the criteria for measuring them. Many educators believe that the use of behavioral terms is actually advantageous to children. Objectives must be so clearly stated that caregivers know the specific purposes of activities conducted with children and can make these known to the children at levels youngsters can comprehend.

The "goal-free" evaluation model[4] was developed by
Scriven. His concern was that evaluators were biased by the
goal statements of the program developer. By measuring the
outcomes of the program against the needs of the population
served, Scriven hoped to create a less contaminated form of
evaluation. Goal-free evaluation is conducted by someone
unfamiliar with program goals, who collects data about the
effects of various components. Scriven points out that goal-
free evaluation can only affect change in a program if participants agree that there has been an accurate description
of the results.

Goal-free evaluation can also be a useful tool for the
day care administrator. It has been previously suggested
that a director, even members of the staff, may have too
great a personal investment to objectively study all aspects
of the program. Scriven's model provides a format for outside input and new perspectives of program outcomes. Many
in the field believe that opportunities for change should
come from as many sources as possible.

Robert Stake, developer of the responsive model of
evaluation[5] had in mind an assessment system found more on

---

[4]Michael Scriven, "Prose and Cons About Goal-Free Evaluation," The Journal of Educational Evaluation, No. 3, 1972.

[5]Robert Stake, "Responsive Evaluation," in David Hamil-
ton, et al. Beyond the Numbers Game: A Reader in Educational
Evaluation. London: Macmillan Education Ltd., 1977.

program activities than program goals. The responsive model requires that the issues for program participants be identified in advance of the evaluation process and considered in presenting the results of evaluation. This model uses a variety of observers to gather data about the program and compiles these into short reports to be presented to participants. Those individuals then provide feedback to the evaluator based upon their values with regard to the program.

The most obvious benefit to day care programs of the responsive model is the opportunity it provides for input from children, staff, and parents. The responsive model enables all of those involved in the program to contribute their thoughts and feelings regarding program successes and failures. A disadvantage may be the ability of those persons to deal with the evaluator's findings. Some persons may be uncomfortable with open expression of the program's flaws. Nonetheless, responsive evaluation represents another potential mode of program assessment.

The accreditation model is perhaps the oldest modern evaluation system, having first been developed in 1871. First designed to screen high schools for admission to a select group of academically approved programs, such systems are now used to assess the qualities of colleges as well as secondary schools. Accreditation models set forth standards for educational programs in the areas of regulation of facilities, qualifications of staff, curriculum, and other resources for instruction. Applying educational institutions are measured against predetermined quality criteria.

The early childhood education already has an accreditation model in place for day care centers. The National Academy of Early Childhood Program's Center Accreditation Project is sponsored by the National Association for the Education of Young Children.[6] Although it is an involved process, which carefully scrutinizes every aspect of child care programs and is voluntary, it has also provided uniformity of standards for the first time in the modern day care arena.

Whatever the model for evaluation or techniques chosen, there are many areas of the day care program that should be scrutinized in the assessment process. The first of these is the center's administration. Study of management effectiveness includes examination of the clarity of program philosophy, achievement of goals and objectives, supervision and coordination of all program components, and effectiveness of communication with staff and parents. An administrator's appropriate management of the center budget is also a consideration.

---

[6]"NAEYC's Center Accreditation Project: Goals and Philosophy," Young Children, Vol. 38, 1983, pp. 33-36.

The educational component has a wide array of facets. Evaluation should consider the learning environment, materials and equipment employed for curriculum implementation, curriculum content and strategies for teaching, and the developmental progress of children. Some of the tools used for assessing the education component are extensive child health and family histories as well as regular observations of children conducted in a variety of learning situations.

Parent involvement should be evaluated in terms of the component's ability to promote family participation at a variety of levels (see Chapter IV). The occasions and number of hours spent by parents in at-school and home-based involvement activities should be carefully recorded throughout the year. In addition, home-school events and the many forms of teacher-parent communication should be documented to simplify assessment procedures. Parents, themselves, must be sought out to give input to any evaluation conducted.

The day care component for staff development should also regularly be studied. A training and development plan for both individuals and the group, assembled at the beginning of each fiscal year, provides some criterion for assessment. Staff training (inservice and other), participation in professional conferences, memberships in early childhood organizations, and projects developed for parents, children, and the community should be among the activities studied. The normal staff evaluation process, consisting of an annual or semi-annual appraisal of staff competence is an important part of this process but should not be the sole method of evaluation. Both direct and indirect-service staff should be observed and provided with immediate feedback based on their performance.

Social services and community involvement aspects of programs also require regular evaluation. Offering social service resources for the day care family means developing awareness of family needs as well as making appropriate referrals. Promoting relationships with a wide range of local agencies and businesses should be part of an annual plan for involvement with community resources.

While these do not represent the only areas for evaluation of day care, they are probably the most significant ones. But determination of the components for evaluation is not the only consideration. Another factor in evaluation is selection of the tools used to collect assessment data, some of which have already been briefly alluded to.

One of the most popular and potentially valuable means of program evaluation is observation. Children, parents, teachers, and administrators can all be observed in the processes of play or work at the center. In order for observation to be a valid assessment tool, however, it should be conducted using predetermined criteria. Examples of these include competencies to be demonstrated by children and teachers in the classroom.

Observation is only useful if the data collected is used as a catalyst for change. This means sharing the results of observations with the appropriate persons, such as parents and the caregivers. Records of staff and children based upon observations should be handled confidentially, and the information concerning specific individuals shared only with those concerned.

Checklists can also record the effect of components of the day care program. Checklists consist of lists of skills or desired behaviors, usually on the part of the child, that are watched for by the day care staff.

Rating scales require an observer to make an objective judgment about human behavior and the degree to which it occurs. While they probably should not be eliminated as a recordkeeping device, rating scales are somewhat less reliable ways of data collection because they rely upon the opinion of the observer.

Observations can be recorded on charts and graphs. The most common uses of these are for curriculum, attendance, and child growth records. However, parent participation in school activities, staff involvement in training, center income and expenditures may also be described on charts and graphs.

One non-observational form of data collection is the questionnaire. Carefully selected, closed, or open-ended items can provide information on parent, staff, or community reactions to program components. Once completed, questionnaires require careful analysis, particularly those which seek the personal opinion of each respondent.

A more elaborate method of evaluation requires the use of control and experimental groups of subjects when an evaluator wishes to study the effects of a particular variable. For example, a day care administrator may want to study the impact of some specific teaching techniques on a group of infants. In order to achieve this, infants are separated into two groups: those with whom the special techniques are used (experimental group) and those for whom the usual techniques are used (control group). At the completion of the study, the two groups are compared to determine whether the experimental teaching techniques have affected infant learning.

Many directors can become very creative about collecting data which support goal achievement. Notes or letters of thanks from parents regarding the program should be saved. Requests for services and sources of referral to the program should be kept on file to demonstrate both need in the community for child care and the reputation enjoyed by the center. The professional growth of staff should be carefully documented. All of these, in addition to the models and tools we have discussed, can be used in the evaluation combination best for the individual center.

Evaluation must and can be a priority in the day care community. It is one of the chief means by which programs can be improved and day care can finally be recognized and accepted for its contribution to the child and family.

BIBLIOGRAPHY

Accreditation Criteria and Procedures of the National Academy
of Early Childhood Programs. Washington, DC: National
Association for the Education of Young Children, 1984.

A description of the procedures and standards of the
center accreditation program developed by the National Association for the Education of Young Children. This is the
first system of its kind in the United States for assessing
the quality of early childhood education programs.

Almy, Millie C., and Celia Genishi. Ways of Studying Children
An Observation Manual for Early Childhood Teachers, Revised Edition, 1979.

A comprehensive view of the study of the young child.
Describes the roles of teachers as students of child behavior, techniques and uses of observation, and other tools
for learning about youngsters.

Anderson, Scarsia B., and Samuel Ball. The Profession and
Practice of Program Evaluation. San Francisco: Jossey-
Bass, 1980.

Presents principles of program evaluation and issues in
the developing field. Various methods of evaluation are presented and corresponding procedures described. Charts and
checklists to promote a better group of tasks of evaluation.

Bickman, Leonard, and David L. Weatherford. Evaluating Early
Intervention Programs for Severely Handicapped Children
and Their Families. Austin, TX: Pro-Ed, 1986.

Techniques for use by staff and administrators in the
evaluation of early intervention programs. Examines program
ability to meet family as well as children's needs.

Cohen, Dorothy H., and Virginia Stern. Observing and Recording the Behavior of Young Children, Second Edition.
New York: Teachers College Press, 1978.

Guidelines for observing children's behavior during
various routines, with materials of all varieties, during
dramatic play, and observing language development. One of
the finest volumes available on child study.

Fiene, Richard J. <u>Child Development Program Evaluation Scale</u>.
    Urbana, IL: ERIC Document Reproduction Service, August
    1984.

    Provides two measurement scales, one to ascertain levels
of quality, the other for day care licensing. Areas measured
include administration, curriculum, health, safety, and nutrition, parent involvement, and social services. An instrument is also provided for recording and rating caregiver
performance.

Fowler, William. <u>Curriculum and Assessment Guidelines for</u>
    <u>Infant and Child Care</u>. Boston: Allyn and Bacon, Inc.,
    1980.

    Procedures for developing learning activities for in-
fants and young children. Curriculum areas covered include
language, play, and problem solving. Information is also included on measures of assessment designed to evaluate progress
of children.

Genishi, Celia, "Observational Research Methods for Early
    Childhood Education," In B. Spodek (Ed.). <u>Handbook of</u>
    <u>Research in Early Childhood Education</u>. New York: The
    Free Press, 1982, pp. 564-591.

    This article describes both older child study methods as
well as new techniques for evaluation in early childhood settings. These are tools useful in assessment of child behavior
and development, teacher behavior, and interactions of adults
and children. A rationale for the use of observation is provided and qualitative and quantitative approaches of observing
and recording are discussed.

Goodwin, William Lawrence, and Laura A. Driscoll. <u>Handbook for</u>
    <u>Measurement and Evaluation in Early Childhood Education</u>.
    San Francisco: Jossey-Bass, 1980.

    Discusses the purpose and value of many types of measure-
ment of the skills of young children. Among these observation,
cognitive, affective, and psychomotor measures are described.
In addition, this volume examines the contributions from other
fields of study, such as sociology and anthropology.

Harms, Thelma, and Richard Clifford. <u>Early Childhood Environ-</u>
    <u>ment Rating Scale</u>. New York: Teachers College Press,
    1980.

Evaluating instrument to assess environment, activities, and other aspects of programs for young children. Areas of the program measured include motor and creative activities, meeting of children's social-emotional development needs, language and problem solving experiences.

Hatfield, Loretta M., "Inservice Evaluation in Early Childhood Education," Young Children, Vol. 37, No. 1, November 1981, pp. 59-64.

Looks at both formal and informal measures of evaluating inservice education for early childhood staff. Explains why evaluation of training is important and offers a sample assessment form.

Honig, Alice S., "Evaluation of Infant/Toddler Intervention Programs," Studies in Educational Evaluation, Vol. 8, No. 3, 1982, pp. 305-316.

Discusses the differences in infant-toddler programs which make summative evaluation difficult. Suggests use of formative assessment to assure that program goals are met along the way.

Irwin, Dee Michelle, and M. Margaret Bushnell. Observational Strategies in Child Study. New York: Holt, 1980.

Provides a historical perspective of child observation and theories of child behavior are discussed. Various methods for recording child behavior as well as key observational strategies are described.

Kontos, Susan, and Robin Stevens, "High Quality Child Care: Does Your Center Measure Up?," Young Children, Vol. 40, No. 2, January 1985, pp. 5-9.

Case studies of program evaluation. Implications and suggestions for assessment criteria for day care evaluation.

Lindberg, Lucile, and Rita Swedlow. Early Childhood Education A Guide for Observation and Participation, Second Edition. Boston: Allyn and Bacon, Inc., 1980.

Examines the materials, arrangement, activities, and interactions in the many interest centers and areas found in day care classrooms. Helpful fill-in charts and worksheets are provided to assist the observer in interpreting what is seen.

Mattick, Ilse, and Frances J. Perkins. <u>Guidelines for Obser-</u>
<u>vation and Assessment: An Approach to Evaluating the</u>
<u>Learning Environment of a Day Care Center</u>, Third Edition.
Washington, DC: The Day Care and Child Development
Council of America, 1974.

Provides guidelines and categories for evaluation of
programs, including assessment of the physical setting,
interactions of adults and children, and the curriculum.

McGlone, Clara, and Imogen Trolander. <u>Day Care Home Provider</u>
<u>Assessment Tool</u>. St. Paul, MN: Toys 'n Things Press,
1983.

Designed as a tool for assessing day care provider
skills in areas of management skills, stimulation of sensory
motor development, creation of cognitive environment, and
socio-emotional skills.

McPherson, Adair, "Assessment of Goal Attainment in Child
Day Care Centers," <u>Child Care Quarterly</u>, Vol. 14, No. 4,
Winter 1985, pp. 287-289.

Reports results of a Utah-based study designed to determine the extent to which goal assessment is conducted in child
day care centers. Types of measurement instruments used are
briefly described. Results showed that less than 50 percent
of directors surveyed regularly assess goal achievement.

Pence, Alan R., "Two Worlds of Day Care: The Practitioner and
the Researcher," Urbana, IL: ERIC Document Reproduction
Service, 1981.

An essay available in both English and French discusses
the overlapping of day care practice and research. The North
American research model is called "generational," and the
author points to the growth of research that is community-
based and relevant to practice. Sample of research which
examined practice issues is discussed.

Prescott, Elizabeth, et al. <u>Day Care as a Child-Rearing</u>
<u>Environment: Vol. II</u>. Washington, DC: National Asso-
ciation for the Education of Young Children, 1972.

A volume focusing on the various aspects of the environment as factors in quality day care. Presents the findings of a study which examined the impact of teacher behavior and attitude and structural variables on young children. It is suggested that teachers must be extremely skills- and milieu-oriented to offer a broad range of experiences in order for child care settings to be beneficial to young children.

Rodriguez, Dorothy, and Marilyn Albert, "Self-Evaluation for Family Day Caregivers," Child Welfare, Vol. 60, No. 4, April 1981, pp. 263-267.

An instrument for use by family day care providers in order to assess effectiveness of their caregiving roles. Derived from field-tested criteria. Provides suggestions for improvement of caregiving skills.

Rowe, Dick, "Making Evaluation Work in Child Care," Child Care Information Exchange, November 1978, pp. 5-10.

Provides guidelines for evaluation of day care programs. Suggests easy measures for evaluation and identifies reasons many evaluations fail to produce results.

Snow, Charles W., "Which Is Better for Young Children--Family Day Care or Center Care?", Paper Presented at the Annual Meeting of the National Association for the Education of Young Children, New Orleans, LA, November 14-17, 1985.

Compares the advantages and disadvantages of center-based and family day care using 20 comparative research studies. Comparative factors include effects of each kind of care on overall child development, environmental differences, and the implications for parental selection of substitute care. Results are somewhat conflicting and no significant differences appear in favor of either kind of care.

Spodek, Bernard (Ed.). Handbook of Research in Early Childhood Education. New York: Free Press, 1982.

This extensive volume provides for persons in the field a review of research conducted in early childhood education. Twenty-four topic areas are covered in categories which include research methods, classroom practices, policy, and developmental theory. Many of the contributors are major spokespersons in early childhood education. They include Spodek, Honig, Bushell, and Genishi.

Takanishi, Ruby, "Evaluation of Early Childhood Programs:
    Toward a Developmental Perspective," in Lilian G. Katz,
    Current Topics in Early Childhood Education, Vol. II.
    Norwood, NJ: Ablex Publishing Company, 1979, pp.
    141-168.

Discusses the basis for evaluation of programs for young
children and the need for a development perspective in assessment efforts. The author urges that evaluation be used to
"facilitate the growth" and "enhance the dignity" of children and adults in the program.

Travers, Jeffrey R., and Richard J. Light (Eds.). Learning
    from Experience: Evaluating Early Childhood Demonstra-
    tion Programs. Washington, DC: National Academy Press,
    1982.

An account of the various systems and tools utilized for
the measurement of outcomes of larger demonstration projects
in early childhood education. A history of the evaluation
of such programs is included along with an examination of
traditional approaches to assessment. Recommendations of
alternative forms of evaluation are provided.

PROGRAMS FOR INFANTS AND TODDLERS

As young as is the modern early childhood education movement, younger still is the acceptance that programs for infants and toddlers can make a valid contribution to the lives of babies and their families.* It was only twenty years ago, in the 1960s, that a few centers designed exclusively for infant care and development began to appear. Some of the earliest infant programs were besieged by criticism from those who believed that alternative care posed a threat to child and family development. These concerns have not disappeared entirely. Some specialists remain convinced that the earliest years of life should be spent at home, in the care of mother, father, or extended family.[1]

In the 1980s, infant-toddler centers are flourishing. As more mothers enter or return to the workforce, the need for infant care centers has become an urgent one. At present, data suggest that 48 percent of mothers of children under three years of age are employed outside of the home.[2] According to other predictions, by the year 2000, 80 percent

---

[1]Burton L. White. The First Three Years of Life. New York: Avon Books, 1975, pp. 253-256.

[2]Robert Lindsey, "Increased Demand for Day Care Prompts a Debate on Regulations, The New York Times, September 2, 1984, p. 52.

*While it is true that infant programs existed during World War II and even at the turn of the century, these were programs for emergency situations. The focus was on custodial care.

of families will have two working parents.[3] While some

children are cared for by relatives, babysitters, or nannies,

many parents seek alternative care in the family day care

home or the child care center.

A second factor in the rise of infant day care is the

growth of public interest in infant development and tech-

niques for promoting or accelerating it.[4] Many parents be-

lieve that a developmental push in infancy enables their

child to more effectively compete with others throughout

life and may be instrumental in raising a child's intelli-

gence quotient. Despite evidence which suggests otherwise,

many parents feel pressured to push their babies to achieve.[5]

Parents select developmental programs designed to promote

academic skills and enroll their infants in enrichment classes

in the belief that gains will be reflected in later school

accomplishments. Meanwhile, most experts in infant develop-

ment are more concerned about the growth of basic trust and

beginning social skills as the outgrowth of quality infant

day care.

---

[3]Dennis Meredith, "Day Care: The Nine-to-Five Dilemma,"
Psychology Today, February 1986, p. 38.

[4]Lynn Langway, et al., "Bringing up Superbaby," Newsweek,
March 28, 1983, pp. 62-68.

[5]Gaylen Moore, "The Superbaby Myth," Psychology Today,
June 1984, pp. 6-7.

At the outset, little was known about what constituted a good infant care program. One of the first volumes published on the subject was Keister's, "The Good Life" for Infants and Toddlers (1970). This tiny book described a model infant "nursery center" funded by the Children's Bureau. It provided minimal descriptions of the facility, quality of interactions, play experiences, and health care offered in a program for 22 infants and toddlers. Keister suggested that trends in employment and family life, "... make it feasible as well as necessary that a new look be taken at the possible alternatives for infant care and that quality care be defined and demonstrated."[6]

A second influential volume was Laura Dittman's, The Infants We Care For (1973). It contained a series of articles by infant day care specialists that delineated the goals for, characteristics of, and staffing of infant day care programs.

A more elaborate view of the infant care center was first provided in 1975 by Willis and Ricciuti. A Good Beginning for Babies: Guidelines for Group Care provided the first extensive examination of a model infant care center. In addition to exploring those aspects of day care that had

---

[6]Mary Elizabeth Keister. "The Good Life" for Infants and Toddlers. Washington, DC: National Association for the Education of Young Children, 1970, p. 12.

been previously addressed, Willis and Ricciuti discussed caregiving routines, the relationship of infant play and learning, social-emotional development, and staff training.

In what may be the most far-ranging view of infant day care, Honig and Lally (1981) have written a guide to the training of caregivers.[7] In their exploration of the day care provider's role in enhancing babies' development, these authors pinpointed the essence of quality infant caregiving. Theories of development, observable child behavior, and caregiving tasks have all been integrated into a coherent and cohesive picture.

Infant day care is different from those services provided for preschool or school-age children. One of the reasons that early childhood practicum students sometimes comment in frustration, "I don't know what to do with babies!," is that they have not yet recognized the unique knowledge and skills required for infant caregiving. Although infants have clear physical, cognitive, and psychosocial needs, they lack the ability to verbally communicate those needs to their caretakers. The infant care provider must not only have a working knowledge of child development but also learn to read and interpret the many signals

---

[7]Alice S. Honig and J. Ronald Lally. Infant Caregiving: A Design for Training, Syracuse, NY: Syracuse University Press, 1981.

emitted by babies. Infant vocalizations, facial expressions, and body language all serve as needs indicators.

Many of those who care for older children ask what one could possibly do all day with several small babies. Their view of children's activities is based upon youngsters' abilities to play cooperatively, communicate with words, and walk. It is difficult for some adults to envision the input into infant development that occurs through many ordinary care-giving routines, as well as through specially designed sensory, language, and motor experiences. The key to effective developmental programs for babies lies in their caregivers' understanding of the impact of adult-infant interactions.

Another of the factors which makes infant day care unique is the way in which teachers and other staff must interact with parents. While all working parents have many concerns related to their children, those of the mothers of young infants can be acute worries. Lally[8] tells us that parental feelings of guilt about leaving the child under three can be very disrupting. There may be a sense of sadness, not unlike mourning, that one's child is being reared by others. For some parents there is the disapproval of grandparents,

---

[8]J. Ronald Lally, "Some Common Concerns of Mothers who Work Outside the Home," <u>Zero to Three</u>, Vol. 1, No. 3, March 1981, p. 10.

relatives, and friends to contend with when the infant is placed in day care. This disapproval can be so significant as to rob the parents themselves of important support systems.

Parents find they must turn over favorite caregiving activities to day care personnel, and this can be a painful experience. Some mothers of infants find that they must give up breastfeeding when they return to work. Nursing an infant can be an important contributor to the early maternal-infant bonding process. Ending breastfeeding earlier than desired may seem to the mother like the permanent severing of a link with her baby.

The infant caregiver functions with a daily awareness of the emotional impact of separation on both parents and baby. The workers become comforters and reassurers of mother, father, and child, and as has been earlier suggested, play important roles as facilitators of the family bond.

As a child matures, developmental needs are met through a wide variety of sources and situations. For example: parents, relatives, playmates, and teachers; home, school, religious organizations, and playgrounds are all involved in nourishing the growth of the older child. Infants, however, express and have needs met within a relatively confined arena. Their primary caregivers--parents, grandparents, and child care workers--who must be both attentive and responsive to baby signals.

Alice Sterling Honig, specialist in infant care suggests that infants have the following developmental needs.[9] Babies need to be cuddled and carried in order to develop in them a sense of "emotional well-being." Many psychologists believe that early physical acceptance and body contact can be determinants of a child's success in intimate relationships later in life. Infants also require loving glances and warm, accepting tones of voice from their important adults, according to Honig. These adult behaviors reassure and nourish the positive feelings of the baby about self.

Babies need someone who can correctly interpret their behavior. Understanding that curiosity, experimentation, and practice are the origins of much of what is sometimes labeled "misbehavior" is an important caregiving task.

Infants need age appropriate toys and safe environments play in and explore. Toys should provide opportunities for sory development and skills practice. A safe learning environment is the facilitator of independence, initiative, and the beginnings of autonomy, when babies are guided by responsive adults.

-----

[9]Alice Sterling Honig, "Meeting the Needs of Infants," Dimensions, January 1983, pp. 4-7.

Quality care and interactions with infants and parents are but two of many issues in infant day care. Even those who endorse quality care have expressed their fear of the long-term impact on babies when day care is less than adequate.[10] It may be many years before longitudinal studies of these children can be completed, but earlier research on maternal and sensory deprivation has shown disastrous results for young children.

The cost of infant care is another of the issues facing both the caregiving community and parents who utilize services. Center-based care for infants can cost well over one hundred dollars in parts of the United States, a fee difficult for many parents to afford. Many doubt that even large-scale government subsidy of day care, which appears unlikely, would make infant day care feasible. In response, child development specialists such a T. Berry Brazelton and Edward Zigler have become advocates of a national policy of paid leaves for new parents, as well as other accommodations by employers that would support childrearing responsibilities of working parents.[11]

While some progress has been made in casting light upon the characteristics of high quality day care programs, more

---

[10]Patricia McCormack, "2 Experts Voice Warning on Infant Care Centers," Philadelphia Inquirer, March 17, 1985.

[11]Ibid.

research and model program development is needed. Since
many infants are cared for in family day care homes, additional information is required to determine the qualities of
good care in home-based settings.

Regulation is one way of assuring high-quality infant
care, but a 1981 survey of state regulations showed little
consistency among the states with regard to standards.
Furthermore, licensing does not imply ongoing monitoring of
a program. The National Day Care Study (1979)[12] suggested
that minimal standards for infant day care should include
staff-child ratios of 1:3 for children under two years, and
1:4 for children aged two to three. In reality, few centers
are able to consistently maintain this staffing level due to
staff absences and shortages of qualified substitutes.

The National Association for Education of Young Children
has developed an accreditation system for day care centers
as one means for coping with the quality issue. However,
this is and will probably remain a voluntary participation
program. Even if highly successful, it will take many years
and changes in existing centers to bring programs up to appropriate levels.

_____

[12]Children at the Center: Final Report of the National
Day Care Study, Executive Summary. Cambridge, MA: Abt Associates, March 1979.

Because of the complexities of center licensing and accreditation, many of those who manage day care facilities choose to do so illegally--perhaps as many as 75 percent of family day care homes are not legally licensed.[13] This is an especially serious problem where infant care is concerned, as babies and toddlers are unable to let anyone know when abuse and neglect take place. Parents may assume that all is well while a child may be receiving care that is seriously inadequate or even dangerous. Day care licensing or registration requires at least occasional supervision of sites for compliance with regulations.

Training of infant caregivers is also an issue of some concern to professionals and parents. As opposed to requirements for elementary teachers, teacher certification is rarely required for those who work with infants and toddlers. While some college programs provide course work and even short practice in dealing with infants and toddlers, few attempt to deal with the many practical issues involved in working with babies and families. Caregivers are left to learn from experiences that come primarily after graduation from school.

Until recently there was no statement of those competencies essential for work with children during the first three year of life. The Washington-based Council for Early

---

[13]Carl T. Rowan and David M. Maize, "Day Care in America," Reader's Digest, June 1985, pp. 103-108.

Childhood Professional Recognition, which awards the Child Development Associate Credential to qualified applicants has, however, identified those skills and they have since been built into the Credential Award System.[14] One problem with CDA credentialing is that it is expensive. Many child care workers cannot afford the cost. Also, like NAEYC's Center Accreditation Program, CDA assessment is voluntary. Both of these programs also suffer greatly from lack of public awareness. Many parents, and even the caregivers themselves, remain unaware of these tools for upgrading program quality. Unless parents and professionals can clearly request center and staff involvement with accrediting and certifying programs, changes will come very slowly if at all.

The final infant day care issues to be discussed in this chapter concern directions for research and establishment of policies. One of these possible policies is paid paternity leaves. The National Center for Clinical Infant Programs[15] suggests several others.

---

[14]C.D.A. Assessment and Credentialing Activities. New York: Bank Street College of Education, Fall 1982.

[15]Who Will Mind the Babies?, A Public Policy of the National Center for Clinical Infant Programs. Washington, DC, 1985.

For example, at present, little is known about the child care alternatives utilized by mothers of children six months of age and younger. Research to obtain this information should be conducted, which would also determine the real problems faced by working parents of infants.

The impact of current programs on children and families must also be extensively explored to highlight the results of inadequate care. These data could be used to influence legislative decisions as well as business and foundation involvement in infant day care.

Infant day care is no longer a choice for many families; it is often a dire necessity. Unless professionals, parents, and legislators begin to work together for solutions to this crisis, the impact on children and families may be felt for many years into the future.

BIBLIOGRAPHY

Anselmo, Sandra, and Jane D. Peterson. <u>A Manual for Caregiver</u>
<u>of Infants and Toddlers</u>. San Francisco: R and E Researc
Associates, 1978.

Focuses on the skills and characteristics most desired in
infant caregivers. Describes a typical day with very young
children, useful equipment, and activity plans. Goals for infants and toddlers are listed.

Baily, Rebecca Anne and Elsie Carter Burton. <u>The Dynamic Self</u>
<u>Activities to Enhance Infant Development</u>. St. Louis, MO:
C.V. Mosby Company, 1982.

Examines the role of the infant as an active participant
in own development. Explores baby interactions with the environment and adult-facilitated activities to promote self-
awareness and self-control.

Brown, Catherine Caldwell (Ed.). <u>Infants at Risk: Assessment</u>
<u>and Intervention, An Update for Health Care Professionals</u>
<u>and Parents</u>, Pediatric Round Table:5. Stillman, N.J.
Johnson and Johnson Baby Products Company, 1981.

Assessing aspects of infant development, screening for
developmental delay and other health problems.

Castle, Kathryn. <u>The Infant and Toddler Handbook: Invitation</u>
<u>for Optimum Development</u>. Atlanta, GA: Humanics Ltd.,
1983.

Provides an overview of infant/toddler development and en
vironments which facilitate it. Describes stage-appropriate
activities for children from birth to twenty-four months of ag
in the areas of sensory and cognitive skills growth, muscle de
velopment, and problem solving.

Cataldo, Christine Z. <u>Infant and Toddler Programs: A Guide t</u>
<u>Very Early Childhood Education</u>. Reading, MA: Addison-
Wesley Publishing Company, 1983.

History, theory, research, and various approaches to the care and education of children from birth to age three. Structuring the environment, roles of caregivers, and activities for young children are featured. Features descriptions of various models and competencies appropriate during the first four years of life.

"Choosing Child Care for Infants and Toddlers: Look First at the Caregiver," Zero to Three, Vol. IV, No. 3, February 1984.

Describes the characteristics of the competent caregiver of children from birth to three. Emphasis on the caregiver as cultivator of the infant's social-emotional development.

Competency Standards and Assessment System for Infant/Toddler Caregivers, Washington, DC: C.D.A. National Credentialing Programs, 1984.

Guidelines for application and preparation for assessment by the Child Development Associate National Credentialing Program. Roles of members of the Local Assessment Team.

Connors, Frances P., Gordon G. Williamson, and John M. Siepp. Program Guide for Infants and Toddlers with Neuromotor and Other Developmental Disabilities. New York: Teachers' College Press, 1978.

Discusses the basics of a developmental program, the normal and atypical sequences of development and appropriate strategies for intervention, and curricular applications. Based upon work the National Collaborative Infant Project of the United Cerebral Palsy Associations.

Dittman, Laura (Ed.). The Infants We Care For, Revised Edition. Washington, DC: National Association for the Education of Young Children, 1984.

Contributions from Burton White, T. B. Brazelton and others in the field regarding the characteristics of high-quality programs for babies. Information is provided on staffing, programming, and child health and nutrition. Revised version of an infant care classic.

Evans, E. Bell, and George E. Saia. Day Care for Infants: The Case for Infant Day Care and a Practical Guide. Boston: Beacon Press, 1972.

Established case for quality day care programs for infan
Provides a guide to establishing and implementing a program.

Fowler, William. <u>Infant and Child Care: A Guide to Education</u>
<u>in Group Settings</u>. Boston: Allyn and Bacon, Inc., 1980

The roles of play and stimulation in early development.
The impact of appropriate infant-caregiver interactions on
infant development.

Frye, Douglas, "The Problem of Infant Day Care," In E. F. Zig
and E. W. Gordon (Eds.). <u>Day Care: Scientific and Soci</u>
<u>Policy Issues</u>. Boston: Auburn House, 1982, pp. 223-242

Describes the problems involved in the evaluation of the
effects of infant day care. Reviews major studies conducted
which have examined this issue and concludes that although
quality day care does not appear to harm babies, additional
research in this area is needed.

Gonzalez-Mena, Janet, and Dianne Widmeyer Eyer. <u>Infancy and</u>
<u>Caregiving</u>. Palo Alto, CA: Mayfield Publishing Company
1980.

The role of the caregiver in relation to the attachment
and other developmental needs of the infant.

Greenfield, Patricia Marks, and Edward Tronick. <u>Infant Curri</u>
<u>lum: The Bromley-Heath Guide to the Care of Infants in</u>
<u>Groups</u>, Revised Edition, Santa Monica, CA: Goodyear Pub
lishing Co., Inc., 1980.

Provides curriculum to develop infant senses, goals for
facilitating intentional behavior, language development. Iss
in infant care, such as scheduling, age-mixing, adult-child i
teraction are discussed. A chart of the sequence of behavior
development is included.

Herbert-Jackson, Emily et al. <u>The Infant Center: A Complete</u>
<u>Guide to Organizing and Managing Infant Day Care</u>. Austi
TX: Pro-Ed, Inc., 1977.

Extensive coverage of the processes of planning space fo
infants, providing appropriate adult-infant interactions, sup
vising the staff, and administering the program. Appendices
include sample forms, bibliographies, and equipment lists for
the infant-toddler center.

Honig, Alice S., and J. Ronald Lally. Infant Caregiving: A Design for Training. Syracuse, NY: Syracuse University Press, 1981.

A training program for infant caregivers. Addresses all aspects of infant development, provides theoretical background, use of space and time. Most suited for preparation of those with minimal formal education or training. Common problems occurring in the day care setting are discussed and activities suggested for trainee use with groups and individual children.

Howes, Carollee, and Judith L. Rubenstein, "Determinants of Toddlers' Experience in Day Care: Age of Entry and Quality of Setting," Child Care Quarterly, Vol. 14, No. 2, Summer 1985, pp. 140-151.

Authors have studied the impact of various child care situations on toddler development. Their findings reveal that the adult-child ratio of the day care setting and subsequent degrees of child-caregiver interaction are predictors of the quality of caregiving experienced. Furthermore, stressed caregivers coping with too large numbers of children are less able to engage in positive interactions with youngsters.

Jones, Elizabeth (Ed.). Supporting the Growth of Infants, Toddlers and Parents. Pasadena, CA: Pacific Oaks, 1979.

A collection of essays by persons working in a variety of capacities with infants and toddlers. Emphasis on the philosophy and values appropriate in work with very young children and their parents.

Kilmer, Sally, "Infant-Toddler Group Day Care: A Review of Research," In Lilian G. Katz Current Topics in Early Childhood Education, Vol. II. Norwood, NJ: Ablex Publishing Company, 1979, pp. 69-116.

Examines effects of day care on the health, development, and social-emotional relationships of infants and toddlers. Conclusions showed few differences between home-reared and center-care infants although the author suggests the need for more refined hypotheses in future research studies.

Leavitt, Robin Lynn, and Brenda Krause Eheart. Toddler Day Care: A Guide to Responsive Caregiving. Lexington, MA: Lexington Books, 1985.

Toddler development and the setting, activities, and interactions that enhance it. Appendices contain extensive lists, forms, and bibliographies.

Lurie, Robert, and Roger Neugebauer (Eds.). <u>Caring for Infant</u>
    <u>and Toddlers: What Works, What Doesn't</u>, Volume II. Bel-
    mont, MA: Child Care Information Ex., 1982.

    An overview of infant-toddler program components and issu
Includes sections on administration and additional resources.
Written by leaders in child care for younger children.

Maxim, George W. <u>The Sourcebook: Activities to Enrich Progra</u>
    <u>for Infants and Young Children</u>. Belmont, CA: Wadsworth
    Publishing Company, 1981.

    Activities to enhance the physical, cognitive, social, an
emotional growth of infants and toddlers. Guidelines for observing in early childhood settings are included.

Maxim, George W. <u>The Very Young: Guiding Children from Infan</u>
    <u>Through the Early Years</u>, Second Edition. Belmont, CA:
    Wadsworth Publishing Company, 1985.

    History and theory of early childhood education. Chil-
dren's social-emotional, affective, motor skills, and cognitiv
development are explored. Curriculum areas are described, including growth of basic academic skills, science and social
studies skills, and creativity development.

Miller, Karen. <u>Things to Do with Toddlers and Twos</u>. Marshfie
    MA: Tel Share Publishing Company, 1984.

    Activities to promote the development of children from
twelve to twenty-four months in the areas of cognitive skills,
sensory development, language growth, muscle skills, problem
solving, and social-emotional development.

Moss, Howard A., Robert Hess, and Carolyn Swift (Eds.). <u>Early</u>
    <u>Intervention Programs for Infants</u>. New York: Haworth,
    1982.

    This volume is devoted to the risks and prevention of
mental health problems in infants. Various approaches to prevention and intervention, as well as issues in infant mental
health are discussed.

Provence, Sally. <u>Guide for the Care of Infants in Groups</u>. Ne
    York: Child Welfare League of America, 1975.

    Milestones in infant development. Includes recommendatio
for program planners and caregivers working to promote infant
growth.

Robertson, Audrey, and Beth Overstad. Infant-Toddler Growth and Development: A Guide for Training Child Care Workers. St. Paul, MN: Toys 'n Things Press, 1979.

Focuses on skills building for caregivers in areas of infant-toddler growth and development and creating learning environment. A guide for trainers in the areas of normal growth and development, provision of safe and healthy environment, and selection of appropriate materials and activities.

Smith, Kenneth E., and Anne P. Jaworski, "Physical Environments for Toddlers in Group Care," Child Care Quarterly, Vol. 13, No. 1, Spring 1984, pp. 52-61.

Describes the gap existing between toddler developmental needs and the environments set up for children this age in child care settings. Makes recommendations for changes in milieu to respond to growth needs of toddlers.

Thoman, Evelyn B., and Sharland Trotter (Eds.). Social Responsiveness of Infants, Pediatric Round Table:2. Stillman, NJ: Johnson and Johnson Baby Products Company, 1978.

Describes the infant as a partner in social interactions. Infantile responsiveness and adult views of infants as interactors are explored. The workings of the mother-infant relationship.

Weiser, Margaret G. Group Care and Education of Infants and Toddlers. St. Louis, MO: C.V. Mosby Company, 1982.

Curriculum for child health and development in the infant-toddler years. Discusses history of views of infancy and principles of child development.

Weissbourd, Bernice, and Judith Musicle (Eds.). Infants: Their Social Environments. Washington, DC: National Association for the Education of Young Children, 1981.

A collection of articles on aspects of infancy by some of the major spokespersons in the field of infant development. Emphasis on impact of parents' interactions with babies. Roles of caregivers and others are also described.

White, Burton L. The First Three Years of Life. New York: Avon Books, 1975.

This opponent of day care for infants and toddlers, describes physical, emotional, and cognitive growth stages in language designed for parents. Activities to promote children's development and appropriate materials are discussed.

<u>Who Will Mind the Babies</u>? A Policy Paper. Washington, DC: National Center for Clinical Infant Programs, 1985.

Describes the need for high quality programs for infants and toddlers of working parents. One of a series of policy papers by NCCIP.

Willis, Anne, and Henry Ricciuti. <u>A Good Beginning for Babies: Guidelines for Group Care</u>. Washington, DC: National Association for the Education of Young Children, 1975.

Staff-parent relationships in infant care programs are discussed. Meeting infant needs through routine care, play activities, and assisting in development of self-control is the focus of this volume.

Young, K. T., and E. F. Zigler, "Infant and Toddler Day Care: Regulations and Policy Implications," <u>American Journal of Orthopsychiatry</u>, Vol. 56, No. 1, January 1986, pp. 43-55.

Describes the results of a survey of licensing requirements for infant and toddler day care in 50 states. Reports on the correlation between regulations and the characteristics of high quality care.

Zigler, Edward and Susan Muenchow, "Infant Day Care and Infant Care Leaves: A Policy Vacuum," <u>American Psychologist</u>, Vol. 38, No. 1, January 1983, pp. 91-94.

Urges psychologists to support changes in social policy to promote and facilitate high quality infant care programs and paid leaves for parents.

FAMILY DAY CARE HOMES

While center-based care is indeed a popular form of child care, it is in no way the most popular form. According to the Children's Foundation, 80 percent of children in alternative care are in home-based facilities.[1] The 1981 Final Report of the Family Day Care Home Study reported an estimated 1.3 million family day care providers care for more than five million children daily in the United States.[2]

Unfortunately, family day care is also the most difficult type of care to regulate. While legal requirements for homes vary, some states mandate licensing, while others ask that providers register their homes; these are difficult requirements to enforce. Family day care occurs in a private home, and to some extent compliance with local requirements becomes a voluntary process.

Another of the problems faced by the day care community is the overwhelming lack of training or education among family day care providers. Although some colleges have begun offering certificate programs for those wishing to specialize in this type of care, and the Council for Early Childhood

---

[1]*Family Day Care Bulletin*, October 1983, p. 1.

[2]*Family Day Care Home Study*, Final Report, Executive Summary. Washington, DC: U.S. Department of Health and Human Services, Administration for Children, Youth and Families, pp. 2-3.

Professional Recognition now offers the Child Development Associate Credential to family day care providers,[3] many more caregivers have had no preparation for their work with young children.

Since home child care, babysitting, has long been an accepted practice among women in American communities, the struggle to create family day care professionals has been difficult. In a research study of providers recently conducted by one of the authors, caregivers were asked what education they had received for their role. "Thirteen years as a mother!," was a typical answer.[4] Even among registered licensed family day care providers the belief is persuasive that parenting experience equals child care skills. Although there has been some legislation in recent years to respond to the need for provider training, the problem has not been adequately addressed. Moreover, public attitudes toward family day care providers are not significantly different from attitudes toward caregivers in center-based settings. "Anyone can take care of children!"

---

[3]*Child Development Associate Assessment System and Competency Standards: Family Day Care Providers*, Washington, DC: U.S. Department of Health and Human Services, 1985.

[4]Kathleen P. Watkins, "A Study of Caregiver Competencies in Family Day Care Homes in the Southeastern Region of Pennsylvania: Implications for the Development of Caregiver Training Programs," Temple University, Philadelphia, PA, 1986. Unpublished research.

Despite these concerns, many caregivers provide quality services for the children of working parents. Family day care offers a distinctly different type of care for families, the characteristics of which can meet many needs of both parents and children. Family day care occurs in the home-like setting desirable to many parents. Some mothers and fathers feel that center-based care is too impersonal and fear that their child will not get the one-to-one attention important to achieving maximum developmental potential. Also comforting to parents is the familiarity of routine that usually occurs in family day care homes. The schedules and activities of centers are more foreign and difficult to understand to those not in the field.

The family day care home is often the source of difficult-to-find services for infants, preschoolers who are not yet toilet trained, school-age youngsters requiring before and after-school care, and children with special needs. Family day care often means a mixed-age grouping, not unlike that a child would experience with a large family of siblings. This is an extremely attractive feature in an age of small families.

Family day care is also unlike the care offered in centers in terms of the equipment and materials available. While child-sized furniture and toys to promote development are available in many day care centers, it could be argued that family day care homes offer the types of experiences and materials a child finds at home. Early childhood education experts have stated their concern that preschool learning has become too compartmentalized in some programs. It has been stressed that integrated learning, not unlike that provided by mothers teaching their children, is more effective a method of presenting information to youngsters than the teaching of isolated skills.[5]

The caregiver who operates a family day care home assumes a unique set of roles and responsibilities. That individual is, first of all, a homemaker, who must coordinate caregiving with care and maintenance of her own home. If she has children, the provider must be a mother while acting as a child care worker.

A provider of family day care is also a business manager. As such, she is responsible for keeping records of expenditures and income, as she collects fees from parents for the service provided. As a manager, the family day care provider plans menus for the meals to be served and also purchases the food to be utilized. Supplies, such as diapers, paper towels, crayons and paper, also have to be inventoried and ordered as needed.

---

[5]George S. Morrison. Early Childhood Education Today, Third Edition. Columbus, OH: Charles E. Merrill Publishing Company, 1984, p. 296.

Each provider, except in instances where the home is affiliated with a social services agency, sets the policies,
guidelines, and fees. This function is administrative in
nature. However, the caregiver also functions in a public
relations role, endeavoring to satisfy parental concerns and
soliciting new families.

One of the most difficult aspects of providing family
day care is that the caregiver usually works alone. Many
are unaware of the existence of professional organizations,
thereby lacking even the networking systems that can provide
the support needed. Days are long, often eleven or twelve
hours, without substitute coverage to enable the provider to
take a break or a sick day.

When the home is agency affiliated some of these problems are alleviated. The support group is present in the
form of other providers linked to the agency. Furthermore,
each provider usually works with a supervisor who collects
fees, fields parents' questions, provides feedback and input
on daily routines, and conducts intake procedures for new
families. Sick, vacation, and personal time are provided by
the sponsoring agency, which has substitute providers available. Even equipment and materials are made available.
Still some providers prefer the autonomy that comes with
self-employment and shy away from involvement with day care
agencies.

One of the most striking benefits of family day care is that it tends to be dramatically lower in cost than center-based care. Many of the operating expenses and high salaries associated with larger facilities do not exist, so costs are kept at a more reasonable level.

In recent years those businesses interested in helping to address employers' child care needs have begun to recognize this aspect of family day care. Some companies employ referral agencies to guide parents in need of care to day care homes near residences or offices. Other businesses employ providers who offer a certain number of slots in each home to care for workers' children. Once again, however, adequate staffing, training, and supervision of homes is important if high quality services are to be offered.

In urban areas family day care homes may be located several to a block. Unlike day care centers, which may be more widely scattered, parents can also select home-based care on the basis of location, perhaps near to home or closer to work sites. Having one's child in the "ideal" location; that is, one selected by the parent can be a great stress reliever.

In the search for means to reduce the welfare rolls, there has been a trend in recent years to train persons receiving Aid to Families with Dependent Children to operate family day care homes. Several projects of this sort have been launched in various parts of the country. Some day care professionals are deeply concerned about this direction, feeling that such programs increase the risk that inappropriate individuals will be taking care of children. It is not enough that a provider like children. Essential abilities and skills must be present or be developed that include planning children's daily programs and interpreting children's needs based upon levels of development and other indicators provided by youngsters.

Those implementing these programs must carefully screen individuals selected to participate, provide training by experienced day care professionals or other early childhood educators, and arrange for at least short-term follow-up of those installed as family day care providers.

Operating a family day care home is not a simple process. In addition to the managerial and public relations functions of caregivers, the program planning role is perhaps the most important. Surely it is one that parenting alone does not prepare an individual for. When the all- important synchronous relationship between parents and child develops in infancy the stage is set for the dyad to begin to interpret and react to one another's communications and behaviors. This ability is one that is not necessarily adaptable to a parent's interactions with other unrelated children. Such ability is usually learned through study of child development psychology and other topics. It is based on clear understanding of the needs of individual children and of the group.

While a multi-age setting is both desirous to some parents and can be a positive environment for children, this mingling of age groups also creates the need for the provider to plan for a wider range of needs. Children must be neither bored nor frequently overstimulated if they are to develop optimally.

Although many family day care homes do not utilize formal lesson plans, the day must nonetheless be structured. Children rely heavily upon a sense of order and familiarity with events in order to adjust to the day care setting. A family day care provider must establish and carry out a daily routine that addresses children's needs for cognitive and sensory stimulation, physical activity, and psychosocial growth. Needs for activity and rest must be met and carefully balanced by the caregiver. It is in this fashion that the family day care home appropriately meets child and family needs.

In the very near future the entire day care community must work diligently to assure that networking among caregivers, training, and recognition of professional status occur for the one million family day care providers in the United States.

BIBLIOGRAPHY

Alston, Frances K. Caring for Other People's Children: A
     Complete Guide to Family Day Care. Baltimore, MD:
     University Park Press, 1984.

     A how-to book for the family day care provider.
Addresses health, safety, nutrition needs of children, and
activities to promote child development in the family day
care setting. Strong chapters on development and care of
children of various age groups and working with parents.
No bibliography.

Bryant, Bridget, Miriam Harris, and Dee Newton. Children and
     Minders. Ypsilanti, MI: High/Scope Press, 1980.

     An interesting look at family day care providers
("minders") and their clients. First-person accounts of parent and child reactions to this alternative form of day care.
Problems in existing home care services are discussed.

Clurman, Mary, "Family Day Care: State of the Art," Day Care
     and Early Education, Vol. 12, No. 1, Fall, 1984, pp. 22-
     23.

     Discusses new trends in the networking of providers,
variations in regulation policies across the country, and
the new involvement of business and industry. Pending
legislation and availability of liability insurance are
also described.

Collins, Alice H., and Eunice L. Watson. Family Day Care:
     A Practical Guide for Parents, Caregivers, and Profes-
     sionals. Boston: Beacon Press, 1977.

     An imaginative study of family day care as seen through
the eyes of "givers" and "users." Needs of parents for quality care are described by imaginary mothers. Also discussed
are licensing of family day care homes, training of care providers, and evaluation criteria.

Costella, Kate, et al. Better Baby Care: A Book for Family
     Day Care Providers. Washington, DC: The Children's
     Foundation, 1986.

The first volume devoted to care of infants in the family
day care setting. Includes sections on infant development
and adjustment to the day care home, working with parents,
and creating a learning environment for babies.

Cryer, Debby, et al. Family Day Care. Chapel Hill, NC:
    North Carolina University at Chapel Hill, Frank Porter
    Graham Center, 1985.

    A correspondence course for training family day care
providers. The package includes a trainer's manual and
packets of training materials for providers. This introductory course contains 12 topic units covering child growth and
development, nutrition, health and safety, parent-caregiver
relationships, environmental considerations, program planning,
and meeting special needs, as well as other subjects.

Divine-Hawkins, Patricia. Family Day Care in the United
    States: Executive Summary. Final Report of the
    National Day Care Home Study. Washington, DC: Depart-
    ment of Health and Human Services, Administration for
    Children, Youth and Families, 1981.

    Presents the findings of a four-year study conducted in
Los Angeles, Philadelphia, and San Antonio to determine the
characteristics of family day care as it exists in several
different cultural and geographic settings. Unregulated as
well as licensed homes were studied, as were caregivers,
child characteristics, and activities conducted in the homes.
Various components of this research examined aspects such as
parent involvement and agency-sponsored homes.

Family Day Care Providers: Child Development Assessment Sys-
    tem and Competency Standards. Washington, DC: C.D.A.
    National Credentialing Program, 1985.

    Describes the credential award system, eligibility re-
quirements, and competencies as prescribed by the Child
Development Associate Credentialing Program. Roles of members of the Local Assessment Team are also described.

Food Buying Guide for Family Day Care Homes. Lansing, Michi-
    gan: Michigan State Board of Education, 1984.

    Provides guidelines to enable the family day care pro-
vider to purchase, prepare, and serve nutritious meals for
children in care. Information is provided on food production
and marketing, packaging and grading, techniques for accur-
ately calculating amounts of food needed, and meal pattern
requirements.

Galinsky, Ellen, and William H. Hooks. <u>The New Extended Family: Day Care That Works</u>. Boston: Houghton Mifflin, 1977.

Discussion and analysis of fourteen model programs for ages birth through school-age. Family day care, center-based programs, and corporate-sponsored are included and their respective problems and issues explored.

Griffin, Al. <u>How to Start and Operate a Day Care Home</u>. Chicago, IL: Henry Regnery Company, 1973.

One of the first manuals for family day care providers, this volume covers management scheduling, programming, and parent-caregiver relationships issues. Tips are also provided on child development and behavior management. Written by a former day care provider, the author aimed this book at the person interested in a profitable career that could be conducted from one's home without specialized training.

Jaisinghani, Vijay T., and Vivian Gunn Morris. <u>Child Care in a Family Setting: A Comprehensive Guide to Family Day Care</u>. Cheltenham, PA: Family Day Care Associates, 1986.

Potpourri of everything one needs to know about organizing, operating, and equipping a family day care home. Sample forms, menus, other information are provided.

Lubchenco, Annette. <u>Spoonful of Lovin: A Manual for Day Care Providers: A Comprehensive Resource for Individual Day Care Providers at Home</u>. Bloomington, IN: Agency for Instructional Television, 1981.

Designed as a training guide for providers. Information on child development, the setting, activities, materials to promote growth of children in the family day care home. Provides a daily reference for problems encountered by providers.

Murphy, Karen. <u>A House Full of Kids</u>. Boston: Beacon Press, 1984.

Guide to developing and operating home-based day care. Information on licensing/registration procedures, financing, parent-caregiver interactions, and children's programs. The author presents the case that licensed day care homes are not necessarily safer, more professionally run, or better places for children to be than non-licensed facilities.

Saunders, Minta R., and Betty C. Sherrod. Family Day Care:
    Suggestions, Ideas, Guides. Greensboro, NC: United Day
    Care Services, March 1975.

    One of the few volumes which deals extensively with an
agency-sponsored family day care program. Job descriptions
and application forms for a variety of staff positions are
provided. Complete description of techniques for recruiting
and training family day care providers and information on licensing of homes and forms to be used by the provider or
agency in the child intake process are included.

Seefeldt, Carol, and Laura L. Dittman (Eds.). Family Day
    Care. Washington, DC: U.S. Department of Health,
    Education and Welfare, Office of Child Development,
    1973.

    Guide for parents seeking family day care for their
children and persons considering providing care in their
homes. Also focuses on role of agencies with affiliate
family day care homes.

Strobl, Catherine, and Nancy Van Domelen. Off to a Good:
    Start: Practical Nutrition for Family Day Care. Denver,
    CO: Wildwood Child Care Programs, 1982.

    Basics of good nutrition, balancing the diets of young
children, shopping for a family day care home. Role of nutrition in child growth and development is stressed.

Wandersman, Lois P., "Ecological Relationships in Family Day
    Care," Child Care Quarterly, Vol. 10, No. 2, Summer
    1981, pp. 89-102.

    The results of an observational study of family day care
homes are reported. Attempts to form hypotheses regarding
the characteristics of individual homes which are most fa-
cilitative of children's social and cognitive growth.

West, Karen (Ed.). Family Day-to-Day Care. Mound, MN:
    Quality Child Care, Inc., 1980.

    A practical guide for family day care providers. Dis-
cusses the management aspects of family day care, and provides
an overview of child development, nutrition, discipline, and
parent communications issues. Contributions by providers.

SCHOOL-AGE CHILD CARE

One of the groups in need of additional day care slots
is the young elementary school child. This youngster is
usually over six and under age twelve. So serious has the
problem of the unsupervised primary-grade child become, that
the term "latchkey children"[1] has been bestowed on those who
go home to empty houses and much public attention has been
paid to this issue in recent years. A growing number of children, perhaps as many as 15 million fall into this category,[2]
and there appears to be no simple solution.

Although there has been resistance on several fronts,
many of the nation's school systems have become involved in
providing before and after-school care.[3] The available programs operate in several different ways. While many after-
school, or extended-day programs are based in schools, some
are community-run, and others are staffed and managed by a
sponsoring school district. Both parents and schools benefit
from the use of school space for extended-day programs. Many

---

[1]George S. Morrison. Early Childhood Education Today,
Third Edition. Columbus, OH: Charles E. Merrill Publishing
Company, 1984, p. 168.

[2]"Finances Are the Key to After-School Child Care,"
The New York Times, September 16, 1985, pp. A1-B5.

[3]James A. Levine and Michelle Seltzer, "Why Are These
Children Staying After School? (And Why Are They So Happy
About It?)," Redbook, September 1980.

schools must remain open during child care hours which usually range from 7 A.M. until 6 P.M. Rather than being empty, the building is in use and some revenues are being collected that help to pay utility and other costs. For parents, there is elimination of the need to have the child transported to and from the site where day care is provided.

Family day care and school-based programs are not, however, the only methods of responding to the needs of the latchkey child. The Orange County, Florida, Public Schools have developed a Home-Base Child Care Program. Neighbors of families have been recruited to provide before and after-school care, in the belief that eight to ten hours per day at school are too many.

After-school care may also be a feature of day care programs for younger children. If the center is located near the school, and escort service or transportation is available, this arrangement can work very well for a family. If the child continues to attend the day care center where he received preschool services, this sort of after-school program can provide essential security as the child moves from one learning environment to another. He or she is reassured by familiar caregivers and "comes home" to his center in the after-school hours.

Just as home-based programs provide a home-like atmosphere, those based in schools tend to provide experiences of a developmentally-enriching nature. Help with homework, sports and games, music lessons, arts and crafts projects, even field trips are among the activities provided in programs for school-age youngsters.

The care received by the older child in a family day care home is probably not dissimilar from that experienced at home, with one major addition--adult supervision. When received by the caregiver the child may get a snack, complete homework, play outdoors, or watch television. Many advocates of home-based programs for school-agers feel that the long hours spent in elementary school are enough of a large group situation for the average child, and a care situation that resembles the youngster's own home is preferable.

When they are available, the cost to parents of after school care tend to be reasonable. They may be charged at a sliding scale rate based on income, and consideration may be given to parents who have two or more children in the program.

The primary problem with after-school care lies in the inadequacy of slots available. Suffering from the same stigma as other forms of day care, extended-day programs are not high on the list of national priorities. Many people doubt a need really exists for before and after-school care. Familiar with the funds pumped into recreational programs in some cities and the efforts of YWCAs and YMCAs; aware of Boy and Girl Scouts and 4-H programs; and aware of the extensive sports programs

available at many schools, they can not imagine that more
after school programs are needed.

Employers may be the most familiar with the latchkey
child dilemma, for every day at approximately 3 P.M. in offices
and factories all over the country, work comes to a halt and
telephone lines are jammed as millions of parents call home
to check on their children. Many parents complain that their
concern for their children's safety interferes with their degree of productivity on the job. They fear for their child's
ability to respond to strangers, unwanted telephone calls,
or household emergencies such as fire, burglary, or illness.

Another of the reasons that school-age programs have been
difficult to implement revolves around professional and legal
arguments about the provision of day care on school property.
Some elementary school educators have argued strenuously
against the assumption of any more of the "responsibilities
of the family." These persons feel that parents have already
abdicated many of their childrearing duties to the schools.

In some states, a hard line is taken by differentiating
day care (not the role of the school) from the extended-day
programs (permissible only during the school's regularly
scheduled days and times of operation).[4] The result has been
after-school programs closed on school holidays and vacation

---

[4]Ibid.

times. This may seriously affect the families in need of services.

Funding is also an issue of some concern. Until recently, many public schools have absorbed the costs of after-school programs. Increasingly, however, resistance is developing to this practice.[5] One of the chief reasons has been the change to Block Grants to transfer funds to the states. Since the federal government urges states to respond to day care needs at the local level, and states tend to make school-age day care a low priority, it has remained just that. The financing issue is further complicated, according to Michelle Seligson of the School-Age Project at Wellesley College, by a lack of research to determine the number, types, and costs of existing child care programs.[6]

Some hope does, however, exist for additional school-age programs. Several non-profit agencies with affiliate groups across the country have taken up the banner of the latchkey child. In 1985, the United Way provided $40 million for day care programs, an increase of $14 million since 1982.[7] The Boy and Girl Scouts of America and Boys and Girls Clubs have been actively involved in after-school care issues and program

---

[5]"Finances Are Key to After-School Child Care," The New York Times, September 16, 1985, pp. A1-B5.

[6]Ibid.

[7]Ibid.

development. In 1986 nearly $5 million was allocated at the federal level to develop school-age programs.

In Texas, a Houston Committee for Private Sector Initiatives that has involved as many as 30 corporations in school-related issues has found ways to respond to child care needs.[8] These include 82 extended-day programs.

While these efforts on behalf of school-age children have been successful, they only begin to scratch the surface of the latchkey problem. Many children, having been warned repeatedly about strangers, live in fear during their hours alone at home. They are afraid to answer the door or telephone, and many have been warned to lie about their parents' presence to any callers.

A child at home alone risks accident, illness, or injury without adult supervision. Having been cautioned frequently about the dangers of fire, water, and electricity, the latchkey child may also fear a mistake that could result in injury to himself and damage to his home. Mostly, he fears disappointing his parents through inappropriate handling of responsibility.

It is responsibility that is at the very heart of the latchkey child's dilemma. He is asked to assume it, rather than enjoy the play and games of childhood. He is forced to

---

[8]Ibid.

take care of himself, and perhaps siblings as well, when someone should be taking care of him. He may have to resort to television viewing for entertainment, because he's told not to leave the house, even to go into the yard.

If this sounds even faintly like a condemnation of the working parent, it is, most emphatically not. For many working parents the choice to work or stay at home is not a choice at all. Economics demand that parents be employed in most American households. It is these same families that have fewer choices where school-age child care is concerned. Somehow, day care seems more critical to many during the preschool years. Once the child reaches school-age fewer programs are available in the community, and the parent must hope the child will be able to manage on his own.

Even though some communities have created after-school hotlines in an attempt to respond to some of the children's needs and fears, these are not enough. A voice on the telephone does not take the place of human companionship, and the future of the latchkey child is the responsibility of the entire country.

Since 1979 the School-Age Child Care Project at Wellesley College has been at the forefront of the movement to respond to the child care needs of older children.[9] With

---

[9]SACC Newsletter, Vol. 1, No. 1, Winter 1983, p. 1.

funding from a broad range of private foundations, the Project has been instrumental in the processes of identifying need, conducting research, and developing demonstration models. The five components of the School-Age Child Care Project are as follows:

A research component identifies model programs throughout the United States, including those operated by the communities, public schools, and in family day care homes.

The component for information, referral, and technical assistance provides individuals, schools, or groups with referrals to programs nationwide as well as offering program development assistance.

A training component develops and conducts courses and workshops for school-age staff in the Wellesley, Massachusetts, area as well as statewide in Massachusetts.

The demonstration feature has supported the development of demonstration sites throughout the United States. These include programs in California, Virginia, and New Mexico as well as other locations.

Finally, the Project has contributed significantly to the literature on school-age child care through its publications. Volumes published include policy reports, an Action Manual, and a legal guide (see bibliography). The Project has sponsored legislation and national conferences and publishes a newsletter related to school-age issues that is read throughout the country.[10] It is with the support of such programs that the child care needs of the older youngster are finally and effectively being addressed.

---

[10]_Ibid_.

BIBLIOGRAPHY

"An After-School Program," in Ellen Galinsky and William H.
     Hooks (Eds.). The New Extended Family: Day Care that
     Works. Boston: Houghton Mifflin, 1977, pp. 173-187.

     Describes the after-school programs successfully oper-
ated in New York City by the Chinatown Planning Council with
the Chinese Garment Manufacturers Association. Includes descriptions of the goals for the program, admissions process,
caregiving staff, child grouping, and problems encountered.

1968 After-School Resources Catalog. Nashville, TN: School
     Age Notes, 1986.

     Lists books written about programs and curricula for the
school-age child.

Bacchus, Joan, and Marsha Hurst. Afterschool. New York: The
     Resourceful Family, 1983.

     A guide for parents seeking care for school-age children
during non-school hours. Provides both selection criteria
and information on individual programs located in the city of
New York. Hours of operation, enrollment, activities, and
eligibility requirements for programs are described.

Baden, Ruth Kramer, et al. School-Age Child Care: An
     Action Manual. Boston: Auburn House, 1982.

     Outlines the processes for setting up school-age child
care programs. Discusses elements of program management and
curriculum development based upon research and program development at the School-Age Child Care Project of Wellesley
College. Appendices are provided on legal and other issues.
Presents a partnership model for school-age programs involving collaboration among agencies, school, and college.

Bender, Judith, Charles H. Flatter, and Barbara Schuyler-Hass
     Elden. Half a Childhood: Time for School-Age Child
     Care. Nashville, TN: School Age NOTES, 1984.

An advocacy manual for school-age child care. Points out the emotional disadvantages and even the dangers of children going home to an empty house. Four levels of care for school-age children, from the minimum to maximum level of acceptability are described. Recommendations for providing school-age day care are also included.

Bergstom, Joan M. _School's Out-Now What? Creative Choices for Your Child_. Berkeley, CA: Ten Speed Press, 1984.

Assistance for parents attempting to plan and structure their children's non-school hours. Topics include extended-day care programs, child safety at home and in the neighborhood, and developing independence. Extensive appendices of resources on organizations books and other helps for parents.

Blan, Rosalie, et al. _Activities for School-Age Child Care_. Washington, DC: National Association for the Education of Young Children, 1977.

Scheduling school-age programs and appropriate use of routines is discussed. Block play, arts and crafts, dramatic play, and science activities are among the types of activities explored. Lists of materials and equipment, discussion stimulators and numerous activity ideas are provided.

Carter, Denise, "The Crisis in School-Age Child Care: What You Should Know. What You Can Do," _PTA Today_, Vol. 10, No. 6, April 1985, pp. 4-8.

Proposes suggestions for the involvement of parent-teacher associations and schools in response to the needs of children in self-care. Problems of latchkey children are discussed.

Cohen, Abby J. _School-Age Child Care: A Legal Manual for Public School Administrators_. Wellesley, MA: School-Age Child Care Project, Wellesley College, 1984.

Reviews and discusses the legal considerations of principals whose schools sponsor or host child care programs. Concerns regarding the legality of schools as sites for day care are discussed. Other chapters deal with topics such as special needs and school board policies.

Cohen, Donald J., et al. _Day Care 4: Serving School-Age Children_. Washington, DC: U.S. Government Printing Office, 1972.

Describes processes for planning and implementing programs for school-age children in public school and community center settings. Suggests program components to address needs of this age range.

Connolly, Frances T., and Cleo Figgures, "School-Age Program: Unique Approaches to Using Community Resources and Technical Summary: Evaluation of the Child Care Program 1982-1983, Paper presented at the School-Age Child Care; It Works! Conference, Vienna, VA, April 12-13, 1984.

A description and summary of the evaluation for fiscal years 1982-1983 of the Child Care Programs of the School District of Philadelphia, Philadelphia, PA. Development of program graduates, volunteer hours recorded, and social service contacts initiated are reported in the attached tables. The program summary describes the history, funding, program components and resources utilized by the school-age program.

Coolsen, Peter, et al. When School's Out and Nobody's Home. Chicago, IL: National Committee for the Prevention of Child Abuse, 1984.

Describes the impact on school-age children of working parents, findings of research on children in self-care, the availability of programs to care for school-age children, and directions for persons interested in developing school-age programs.

Eller, Carollee, et al. The Hours We Can't Be Home: Developing a School-age Child Care Program. A Handbook for Parents. Hartford, CT: Collaboration for Connecticut's Children, 1985.

A guide to planning and implementing school-age child care written for parents. Information on conducting needs assessment and identifying the appropriate program for the community are provided. Discusses policy development, staffing, and budgeting. Appendices contain forms that can be adapted for use by developing programs.

"Finances Are Key to After-School Child Care," The New York Times, September 16, 1985.

Explores the latchkey child dilemma and suggests that the U.S. government hopes for local rather than federal responses to the need for after-school child care.

Kearney, Shery S. (Comp.). <u>Caring for Our Children: Day Care Issues Facing the States</u>. Lexington, KY: States Information Center, The Council of State Governments, 1984.

A report describing the activities of state governments in recent years around the issue of school-age child care. Programs for state employees' children, changes in government policies and standards for programs, and state grants for school-age programs are among the changes discussed.

Kolb, Sandra, and Anne Strickland, "Today I Dance: What Children Want After School," <u>Day Care and Early Education</u>, Vol. 12, No. 3, Spring 1985, pp. 19-21.

Describes results of a survey of 100 children ages five to nine years to inquire about what they most enjoy as after-school activities. Children reported that unstructured outdoor play, play with friends, sports, dancing, and field trips were their primary choices. The implications for after-school settings, activities, and staffing are discussed.

Kyte, Kathy S. <u>In Charge: A Complete Handbook for Kids with Working Parents</u>. New York: Random House, 1983.

Designed to assist the working family as they plan their children's self-care hours. Provides children with information on handling emergencies and responding to a range of everyday situations that might occur while they are alone at home.

Long, Lynette, and Thomas Long. <u>The Handbook for Latchkey Children and Their Parents</u>. New York: Arbor House, 1984.

Coverage of the pros and cons of the latchkey issue. Includes case studies of individual children and how self-care time is spent. Problems encountered by youngsters as well as feelings, needs, and successes are discussed.

McNairy, Merion R., "School-Age Child Care: Program and Policy Issues," <u>Educational Horizons</u>, Vol. 62, No. 2, Winter 1984, pp. 64-67.

Urges involvement of educators as advocates for school-age child care. Discusses the need for programs and cooperation of schools and other concerned groups.

Nall, Susan W., and Stephen E. Switzer. Extended-Day Programs
in Independent Schools. Boston: National Association
of Independent Schools, 1984.

A three part volume which presents the findings of a
survey of before-and-after school programs in private schools.
Profiles of seven extended day programs are included.

Neugebauer, Roger. "School Age Day Care: Developing a Responsive Curriculum," Child Care Information Exchange,
January 1980, pp. 17-20.

Discussion of techniques for responding to the developmental needs of school-age children through a child care
program.

Neugebauer, Roger. "School Age Day Care: Getting It Off The
Ground," Child Care Information Exchange, November 1979,
pp. 9-15.

Steps to the organization and implementation of school-
age day care. Suggestions for needs assessments, recruitment
of families, and budgeting initial costs are included. A
good although dated bibliography follows.

Neugebauer, Roger, "School-Age Day Care: Selecting and
Motivating Staff," Child Care Information Exchange,
November 1980, pp. 27-31.

Ideas for selecting, motivating, and increasing the
productivity of staff in after school-program settings.

Osborne, Linda B. Family Day Care Check-In Program: After
School Care for Children Aged 10-14. Washington, DC:
Department of Health and Human Services, 1982.

Describes an after school, family day care program for
children ages 10 to 14 years operating in Fairfax County,
Virginia. The program is designed to be replicated and
sponsored by community groups. Information on training of
caregivers and children's participation in planning their
own activities is provided. Two booklets are provided in
this set.

Rothman, Sheldon L., "Latchkey Children: A Bibliography,"
Education Libraries, Vol. 10, No. 1, Winter 1985,
pp. 12-16.

An annotated bibliography on children in self-care con-
taining 31 items. Includes reports of eight school-age day
care programs and guides for designing programs to meet the
needs of the latchkey child.

School-Age Child Care Project, "School-Age Child Care," in
E. F. Zigler and E. W. Gordon (Eds.). Day Care: Scientific and Social Policy Issues. Boston: Auburn House,
1982, pp. 457-475.

Offers a history of care for the school-age child. Provides descriptions of current programs and practices and suggests directions for the future. Concerns expressed include
the needs to improve the public image of day care, provide
staff training, and finance additional programs.

School-Age Day Care Study: Executive Summary. Washington,
DC: Office of Program Development, Department of Health
and Human Services, 1983.

Reports data on school-age child care programs in Virginia and Minnesota for fiscal year 1981-1982. The purposes
of the study were to identify the child care alternatives
utilized among various families; determine the degree of parental satisfaction with care; identify methods employed by
parents to identify services; describe the circumstances under
which children are in sibling or self-care; and describe the
various ways in which child care needs are addressed by the
community.

"School Facilities Child Care Act. Hearing before the Sub-
committee on Education, Arts and Humanities of the
Committee on Labor and Human Resources," United States
Senate, Ninety-Eighth Congress, Second Session on
S. 1531 to Encourage the Use of Public School Facilities
before and after School Hours for the Care of School-
Aged Children and for Other Purposes, April 27, 1984.

Proceedings of hearings held in Pinellas County, Florida, site of the nation's largest before and after school
program. Testimony of children attending programs is included. The need for government support of school-age child
care and benefits of programs are presented.

Seligson, Michelle, et al. School-Age Child Care: A Policy
Report. Wellesley, MA: Wellesley College, Center for
Research on Women, 1983.

Designed for those instrumental in developing policy and
programs relative to the child care needs of school-age children. Includes a history of school-care in the United States,
research findings, roles of public schools in providing before and after-school care, and recommendations for policy
makers. Appendices include program models, a chart comparing
the budgets of three programs, and a comparison of states'
day care licensing standards, as well as other helpful information.

Spence, Helen P., and Patricia N. Adams. <u>Family Day Care:</u>
<u>Children Growing and Learning in a Home Environment</u>.
Wellesley, MA: Massachusetts Bay Community College,
Wellesley Division of Continuing Education and Commun-
ity Services, 1980.

Results of a family day care training program conducted
at Massachusetts Bay Community College. Sections covered
address topics such as the importance of day care for children and parents; preparing one's home and family to provide
day care; child development; and activities for various age
groups.

Strommer, Ellen A., et al. <u>Developmental Psychology: The</u>
<u>School-Age Child</u>, Revised Edition. , Homewood, IL:
Dorsey Press, 1983.

An overview of development during middle childhood, including physical, psychosocial, and cognitive growth. Results
of research and clinical activity are presented. Personality
theory, intelligence tests, and moral development are also
discussed.

Swan, Helen L., and Victoria Houston. <u>Alone After School</u>.
Englewood Cliffs, NJ: Prentice-Hall, 1985.

Addresses the issue of the child in self-care. Ideas
for both children and parents to plan hours spent without
supervision and respond to problems which might arise.

DIRECTIONS FOR PROFESSIONALISM

Day care providers, along with other early childhood educators, have long been immeshed in a struggle for professional recognition. The battle is occurring on several fronts, a problem which makes the evolution of strategies a complex process. On one hand, there is the public view of child care programs. This impression combines the confused elements of "caregiving as babysitting" and "child care programs as social services for the disadvantaged." One might effectively argue that as an increasing number of families utilize day care services, the latter view is gradually disappearing although there is little evidence that the value placed on child care workers has increased in recent years.

The second arena of concern stems from the attitudes of colleagues in other areas of education. Day care is perceived to be in a less important realm than elementary or secondary education. Even at a time when the importance of early learning is clearly understood, those who function as skilled facilitators of child growth and development are not perceived as specialists but as surrogate parents. The gap is further widened by the strict adherence of non-early childhood educators to policies of decreased involvement in family issues, a role understood and accepted by day care staff.

Complicating the public relations issue is confusion in the ranks. Some child care personnel, including day care staff, would prefer to be viewed as a field separate from early childhood education.[1] Indeed, when one looks at the range of caregiving versus early childhood positions, there is sometimes considerable difference in responsibilities and roles. At times, the individual in the day care setting seems to be living in two worlds, belonging to both (or neither?) professions. It may be said that the day care provider suffers from an identity crisis.

Two of the qualifications of a discipline are an established body of literature and accepted paradigms for the field.[2] While this volume demonstrates the existence of information and research devoted to day care, the major spokespersons and propositions in this area tend to be borrowed from child development and psychology.

Confusion also permeates the expectations for day care workers in practice. Marian Blum may have said it best:

> Day care is an institution that demands of its staff a two-fold, paradoxical role: professional and menial. Raise our children, parents ask, according to the best theories of Freud, Erikson, and Piaget. Make them healthy, secure, intelligent, challenged, social, happy, ambitious, talented, gentle, competent, loving,

---

[1]Norman Powell et al., "Professional Growth through Partnership Between a National Organization and a University," _Child Welfare_, Vol. LXIV, No. 2, March-April 1985, p. 166.

[2]Thomas S. Kuhn. _The Structure of Scientific Revolutions_, Second Edition. Chicago, IL: University of Chicago Press, 1970.

> independent, and mature. While you are
> doing that, please change their diapers,
> toilet train them, keep track of their
> stray socks and their lost teddy bears...
> please sweep the floors and clean the
> potties and take out the garbage... But
> please don't ever charge me more than
> two dollars an hour.[3]

While Blum elaborates with many examples of the low regard of both professionals and the public for child care
workers,[4] the problem is more extensive than many in day
care are willing to recognize or admit. Many day care providers are highly skilled, trained individuals, but many are
not. Some lack formal preparation for their work with young
children or are unable to translate theory into practice.
Even the journals and periodicals for clinicians continue to
list "...warmth, patience, and enjoyment" of children as among
the crucial competencies for caregivers.[5] As long as the profession itself describes essential caregiving skills in emotional terms, how can the public and colleagues in other areas
of education be expected to respect the day care provider's
expertise?

---

[3]Marian Blum. The Day Care Dilemma: Women and Children
First. Lexington, MA: Lexington Books, 1983, p. 41.

[4]Ibid, pp. 42-43.

[5]"Choosing Child Care for Infants and Toddlers: Look
First at the Caregiver," Zero to Three, Vol. IV, No. 3, February 1984.

Another of the gray areas in the professional development of caregivers is that of the components of teacher training programs. College programs for early childhood educators tend to prepare individuals for kindergarten and primary school teaching. Instead of focusing on the underlying cognitive and other skills which make a child's later performance in curriculum content areas possible, the emphasis is on content areas. As a result, graduates of these departments may have inappropriate expectations for young children or be unable to explain to parents the reasons that children's play constitutes learning experience.

Another drawback of college programs is the usual lack of field experience. Although there are some exceptions, most early childhood departments limit the amount of time spent by preservice teachers in practice settings to two or three semesters per program. Once employed, child care workers find that familiarity with curriculum does not prepare them for the myriad of behaviors, levels of development, and learning styles encountered in the classroom. In addition, college programs prepare persons to think of themselves as performers in the traditional mode,[6] when the reality is

---

[6]Seen as the well-groomed teacher with a classroom full of polite, nicely-dressed, and well-behaved children parented by properly respectful mothers and fathers.

more like that described by Blum. For some day care workers, the reality is too harsh and burnout quickly sets in.

Recently, the major early childhood organizations have taken steps to develop guidelines for teacher training.[7] Furthermore, the Council for Early Childhood Professional Recognition, which awards the Child Development Associate Credential, has gained a wider acceptance even to the point of inclusion in state standards for day care center personnel.[8] Unfortunately, adoption of these guidelines and the Credential still tends to occur on a voluntary basis. Enforced standards for programs generally deal with the state of the facility, child health, and safety issues. Given the trend toward non-intervention by the federal government and the autonomy of American universities, it is also unlikely that any agreement about large-scale training requirements for day care providers will occur in the near future.

Among the more serious needs of day care personnel is that one for adequate support systems to offset "professional

---

[7]National Association for the Education of Young Children and Association for Childhood Educational International.

[8]Jones, Leroy, et al. The Child Development Associate Program: A Guide to Program Administration. Washington, DC: U.S. Department of Health and Human Services, Office of Human Development Services, 1981.

lonliness"[9] and stress. Long hours spent responding to human needs, inadequate teacher-child ratios, and low salaries add up to tensions that can affect the quality of caregiving. Maslach[10] and others have documented the stress dilemma and its impact among the children and adults in child care settings. The degree of stress may be indicated by frequent staff illness or other absence, classroom management problems, or interpersonal issues. Stress situations may be accentuated by a lack of networks or support systems for caregivers and other staff.

Professional loneliness may be defined as an absence of associates with whom to share the pleasures and disappointments of one's career. The more dedicated and involved individuals are in their work, the greater the need for support systems. Day care providers and others in the human service professions deal with the feelings, needs, and behaviors of others at an intense level on a daily basis. Not only must these professionals accept the actions of clients but they must constantly be reacting in appropriate ways. Caregivers

[9]Lucius Durant, Jr., and Kathleen Pullan Watkins, "Developing Professional Partnerships in Early Childhood Settings," Target I. Amarillo, TX: Teaching Pathways, Inc., 1983.

[10]Christina Maslach and Ayala Pines, "The Burnout Syndrome in the Day Care Setting," Child Care Quarterly, Summer 1977, 6, pp. 100-13.

may be left feeling robbed of their individuality and recognition of their own needs, like machines that must keep functioning even when overtaxed. Such feelings may be heightened if caregivers are also spouses and parents themselves, and the giving continues unabated after work hours. The need to share professional concerns may go unaddressed.

One way to respond to the problems of stress and professional loneliness is to promote the growth of professional partnerships among day care staff.[11] These consist of formalized agreements by co-workers to engage in mutually and individually supportive activities to facilitate their growth as caregivers. Partners agree to work toward common goals, share experiences, and remain loyal to one another. Willingness to compromise, common language, and frequent communications are some of the other components of partnership. Such associations demand discretion, trust, and agreement to refrain from blaming one individual in times of stress or failure to achieve goals.

The family day care provider who works independent of a child care agency may be particularly vulnerable to stress. This individual may work longer hours, as many as fifteen a day, than the center-based caregiver without other staff to diffuse the demands of children and parents. Many of those

---

[11]Lucius Durant, Jr., and Kathleen Pullan Watkins, "Developing Professional Partnerships in Early Childhood Settings," Target I. Amarillo, TX: Teaching Pathways, Inc., 1983.

managing day care homes do not have the luxury of sick or
vacation days. For these reasons, steps have been taken in
many areas of the country to develop family day care networks. A newly-formed national, professional group[12] as well
as efforts by colleges, day care referral systems, and other
social service groups aim at tying together the vast numbers
of caregivers operating home-based programs.

One of the most grievous problems faced by the day care
community is the recent wholesale response by the public to
the need for day care. In such cities as Philadelphia everyone
is considering going into the child care business and, despite
an overwhelming lack of preparation or training, many individuals are doing just that. In storefront spaces and homes,
church basements, and community centers, day care centers are
opening by the hundreds. Some see child care as a money-
making scheme. Others use day care to write off taxable
monies earned in other ventures or jobs. What is most tragic
is that these individuals seldom lack clients. There are
probably two reasons for this lack of discrimination in the
selection of day care services. The first is the desperation
experienced by some families when they realize that quality
child care is difficult to find. Yet another factor is the

---

[12]National Association for Family Day Care, P.O. Box
5778, Nashville, TN 37208.

tendency to measure facilities in terms of decor and materials rather than the quality of caregiving. Simply put, most parents do not know what to look for in a day care center.

The confusion regarding day care expertise is further complicated by the media. Even in large cities where many programs, training institutions, and other avenues for information on day care abound, many television and radio stations interview pediatricians, psychologists, or other so-called "experts" about day care issues. Mysteriously, the profession is usually silent when this situation occurs. Unless leaders in day care actively protest the perpetuation of misconceptions about the roles and skills of providers and caregivers, little change in public attitude and use of services will occur.

In conclusion, the parameters of directions for professional growth for members of the day care community fall into two major categories.

The first of these concerns the self-view of caregivers in center-based and family day care settings. Not just individuals, but the day care community as a whole must take a hard look at new means to respond to training needs and the need for support systems. At the elementary and secondary school levels, teachers often have unions to help focus attention on their concerns, both among the rank-and-file and among the public. Without the union and other widespread participation in professional groups, even day care workers themselves may be unclear about areas where growth and change may be needed. Concerted effort must be launched to upgrade the understanding of all child care workers about the importance of their roles in the lives of children and families. Without increased comprehension of our own value how can attitudes of the public be changed?

Caregivers as a group must decide to which field they wish to belong--early child education or the newly-formed child care profession. Such lack of agreement, while not appearing to have serious consequences in the present, ultimately undermines day care by interfering with the clear establishment of goals, tasks, and competencies for caregiving personnel.

Scholars, college-level educators, and trainers preparing persons for work in day care settings must come to some agreement regarding components of caregiver preparation. Although, for example, many agree upon the value of the Child Development Associate competencies, others remain unconvinced of the validity of competency-based education. Proponents of the latter view may emphasize a student-caregiver's training in theoretical aspects of caregiving and child development, as opposed to a balance between understanding of theory and demonstration of practical skills. While colleges should maintain some degree of autonomy in program development, there must be some consensus regarding minimal standards for training programs. This need is especially great in lieu of the failure of most states to set any accreditation criteria for caregiving personnel.

The second category for professional direction involves the roles of caregivers as day care advocates as well as child advocates. Media interest in day care issues has had some impact, but much remains to be accomplished in the areas of public awareness and attitude toward child care professionals. Individual day care providers must assume more active roles in informing the public about day care and those who care for young children. The expertise of caregivers must be clearly established both for the sake of those who need services and the benefit of individuals considering making day care their business.

Many have written with concern about the potential ill-effects of poor quality care. They have expressed concern that child development and family relationships can suffer if youngsters are exposed to inferior day care programs. Others lament the decrease in federal funding and deregulation of programs for young children. We can succumb to feelings of helplessness or step up our activities in those areas where we do have control. The genesis for change does not lie with legislators or policy makers but must come from within the day care community itself.

BIBLIOGRAPHY

Ade, William, "Professionalism and Its Impact for the Field of
     Early Childhood Education," Young Children, 37, March
     1982, pp. 25-32.

     Expresses concern that the early childhood profession
has not achieved deserved status because it lacks certain
unique characteristics associated with professionalism.
Significant changes would occur in the field were these
characteristics to be present. It is suggested that attain-
ing professional recognition is a long and difficult process.

Almy, Millie, "Interdisciplinary Preparation for Leaders in
     Early Education and Child Development," Advances in
     Early Education and Day Care, Vol. 2, 1982, pp. 61-89.

     Explores issues related to training child care pro-
fessionals. Criteria for survey of ten college and university programs included integration of theory and practice and
evaluation mechanisms.

Caldwell, Betty M., "How Can We Educate the American Public
     About the Child Care Profession," Young Children, 38,
     March 1983, pp. 11-17.

     Identifies the conceptual and other problems surrounding
the child care profession and make specific recommendations
for long-term changes in public attitude.

Durant, Lucius, Jr., and Kathleen Pullan Watkins, "Developing
     Professional Partnerships in Early Childhood Education
     Settings," Target I, Amarillo, TX: Teaching Pathways,
     Inc., 1983.

     Discusses some of the many factors causing stress and
interpersonal skills problems in day care centers and other
early childhood programs. Suggests development of professional partnerships, a unique form of interaction, as a tool
for enhancing work relationships.

Early Childhood Teacher Education Guidelines for Four and
     Five-Year Programs. Washington, DC: National Associa-
     tion for the Education of Young Children, 1982.

Provides standards for early childhood education teacher training and education programs.

Fernandez, Happy Craven. <u>The Child Advocacy Handbook</u>. New York: The Pilgrim Press, 1980.

An overview of the advocacy role. Characteristics and skills of the child advocate are described, along with roles of child care personnel, parents, and children, themselves. Proposes an agenda for the future of the advocacy movement. Case studies of advocacy efforts are included.

Freudenberger, Herbert, "Burnout: Occupational Hazard of the Child Care Worker," <u>Child Care Quarterly</u>, Summer 1977, pp. 90-91.

Discusses the symptoms of burnout as they appear in day care providers, including cynicism, negativism, inflexibility, and rigidity. The impact is boredom with the children and the work according to the author.

Hostetler, Lana, "Putting Our Child Care Skills to Work in Advocacy," <u>Child Care Information Exchange</u>, January/February 1983, pp. 25-29.

Focuses on roles of child care workers as advocates for young children. The uses of caregiving skills in the advocacy forum are discussed.

Hymes, James L. Jr. <u>Early Childhood Education: An Introduction to the Profession</u>, Second Edition. Washington, DC: National Association for the Education of Young Children, 1975.

History, status, and issues in early childhood education are discussed. Proposes direction for the future of early childhood education.

Jorde, Paula. <u>Avoiding Burnout: Strategies for Managing Time, Space, and People in Early Childhood Education</u>. Washington, DC: Acropolis Books, 1983.

Stress-reduction for day care personnel using techniques for improved time-management, human resources management, and self-assessment. Useful as an administrative tool to maintain program quality and staff job satisfaction.

Katz, Lilian G. <u>More Talks with Teachers</u>. Urbana, IL: ERIC Clearinghouse on Elementary and Early Childhood Education, 1984.

A collection of five new papers based upon Katz' own experience and discussions with others. Issues addressed range from defining professionalism to assessing individual child development.

Katz, Lilian G., and Evangeline H. Ward. <u>Ethical Behavior in Early Childhood Education</u>. Washington, DC: National Association for the Education of Young Children, 1978.

This volume discusses issues faced by teachers and caregivers working with young children. Suggests an appropriate code of ethics for the early childhood educator.

Kenny, Ellen M., and Rebecca Turner Cross. <u>Working Together: A Guide to Interorganizational Collaboration for Child Care Providers</u>. Washington, DC: U.S. Office of Health and Human Services (n.d.).

The various roles of teachers and child care providers in Title XX Day Care, family day care, and Head Start agencies are compared. Barriers to inter-agency collaboration are described, including differences in philosophy, administration, and level of services delivered. Techniques are provided for the development of cooperative relationships among human service providers.

Kostelnik, Marjorie, "Making the Transition from Teacher to Director," <u>Child Care Information Exchange</u>, January/ February, 1982, pp. 11-16.

Emphasizes the enormity of the transition from teaching to the director's role. Provides step-by-step procedures for establishing one's authority in the director's role. Contributions from many administrators.

Maslach, Christina, and Ayala Pines, "The Burnout Syndrome in the Day Care Setting," <u>Child Care Quarterly</u>, Summer 1977, 6, pp. 100-113.

Describes those assets of the day care setting, including staff-child ratios, lack of formalized support systems, and longer working hours, which contribute to stress and burn-out in child care workers.

Seaver, Judith W., Carol A. Cartwright, Cecelia B. Ward, and C. Annette Heasley. <u>Caregivers with Young Children</u>. Washington, DC: National Association for the Education of Young Children, 1979.

Provides a format to enable child care students and others to look at their interests and skills to determine which type of work with children they are most suited to.

Teacher Education Committee, "Preparation of Early Childhood Teachers," A Position Paper. Washington, DC: Association for Childhood Education International, 1983.

Describes the components of teacher training programs for those working with children from birth to age eight.

Vander Ven, Karen (Ed.). Competent Caregivers--Competent Children. New York: Haworth, 1985.

An overview of the issues and trends in the training of child care workers. Provides guidelines for planning and implementing a variety of educational activities, and presents training models.

Westman, Jack C. Child Advocacy. New York: Free Press, 1979.

Strategies for child advocacy in the areas of individual and class advocacy. The need for an interdisciplinary approach to advocacy is discussed. A historical perspective of the advocacy movement is provided.

"Why Do Directors Burn Out?," Child Care Information Exchange, September 1979, pp. 6-8.

Discusses the stresses, low salaries and benefits, lack of support and other causes of burnout in day care directors. Makes suggestions for offsetting burnout.

ISSUES FACING THE DAY CARE COMMUNITY

Despite the increased demand for and interest in day care in the United States, child care professionals face a future with a growing number of questions and concerns. There are issues which color the public's view of day care as well as individual caregivers' self-image. Most importantly, these concerns and the resolutions sought to address them may well determine degrees of growth and development for millions of children and their families. At a time of intense social depersonalization and neglect of the needs of youngsters and their parents, the child care community is gravely conscious of problems of service availability, quality, and policies. These issues have been consistently addressed in professional journals, at conferences, and by the media. To some extent, they have been touched on in this volume. This last essay will attempt to summarize some of the needs and questions as they have arisen and will continue to arise in the last years of this century.

Even as census figures and labor department figures in-dicate the increased need for child care for children from birth to age 14, the federal government continues to decrease its level of involvement as a service provider. Not only has this move created a void in day care availability, but recent changes in the interaction of the federal government with the

states, toward decentralization of power, have impacted negatively on the degree to which day care is regulated and supervised by monitoring agencies.

While some interest has been generated in service regulation by the recent reports of child sexual abuse in day
care centers,[1] the response of the Congress has been typ-
ically remedial. There exists a clear lack of understanding
among legislators that child abuse, in and of itself, is a
symptom (albeit a catastrophic one) of much deeper problems.
The abuse situations, contrary to popular belief, are probably
not widespread, while other symptoms of the lack of regulation
are clearly evident. The public is not stirred to respond to
these problems in the same way as to instances of abuse or
neglect.

When in 1985, Public Law 98-473 allocated $25 million in
Title XX training monies to child care workers, state licensing personnel, and parents, there were conditions attached.
States accepting these funds were charged with the establishment of procedures for checking the employment histories and
criminal records of persons seeking employment in child day
care. Little direction was provided for this process, however. Some of the questions since raised regarding the implications of this law include: Which body or agency will

---

[1]Russell Watson et al., "A Hidden Epidemic," Newsweek,
May 14, 1984, pp. 30-36.

be responsible for overseeing the investigation process? Who will retain information obtained through the Federal Bureau of Investigation? Do rejected applicants have the right to appeal? Which crimes constitute valid reasons to refuse an individual employment?

Cutbacks at the federal level have greatly affected funding and regulation at the state level. Since the implementation of Block Grants, most states must carefully divide the allocated monies between a wide range of human service activities. Annual allocations for day care are generally dependent on the degree of legislative support present and the extent of state-wide lobby for funds. In recent years, 32 states have cut back on the number of staff who monitor programs as well as the standards for some federal and state-funded programs.[2] Some claim this makes it possible for more programs to open and reduces the amount of the financial committment required by the state. Others realize the effect these directions have on the quality of day care programs.

Child Care Information Exchange recently reported that up to 70 percent of all child care centers in the United States are housed in church buildings with more than three million children in care.[3] While some of these programs merely rent space from churches, others are church sponsored. This has

---

[2]Child Care Information Exchange, March 1986, p. 8.

[3]Ibid.

raised another issue of a regulatory nature in some states.
Missouri and Florida are among those states which exempt
church-run day care from state licensing requirements.[4,5]
The American Civil Liberties Union and other non-exempt programs are now challenging those exemptions in an effort to
raise the quality of services provided by church-sponsored
programs.

If child advocates are eventually successful in raising
the standards for child day care programs, who will provide
the funds to enable program developers to meet those standards? Political and economic trends for the last two decades
of this century do not let us anticipate increased financial
involvement.

To a degree the corporate world has become involved in
providing some additional alternatives to meet the child care
needs of employed parents. According to recent data, approximately 150 businesses offer on-site or nearby child care.
Another 2,500 companies offer child care assistance for their
employees, and child care information and referral services
are used by 500 businesses nationally.[6] In Massachusetts,
a pilot program now offers companies low interest loans in

---

[4]"Child Care Law Is Challenged," Education Week, May 28,
1986, p. 2.

[5]"Day Care Lawsuit Fights Exemption of Religious Centers," Education Week, April 23, 1986, p. 2.

[6]Barbara Kantrowitz et al., "Changes in the Workplace,"
Newsweek, March 31, 1986, p. 57.

amounts up to $25,000 if they will set up their own day care programs.[7]

Providing day care on site or near the workplace appears to benefit both the family and employers. When the Department of Labor surveyed employer and union-sponsored programs in 1978,[8] they found that businesses providing child care services reported increased ability to attract workers, lower absenteeism and turnover rates, and improved attitudes of employees toward their work and sponsoring organizations among the favorable results. On-site day care has also been shown to enhance business-community relationships as evidenced through media attention and other feedback.

Employer-supported programs are often helpful in reducing the stress parents associate with other forms of child care. Some parents find that their sitters and other day care arrangements are unreliable. The care provider may be unexpectedly unavailable or suddenly out of business leaving parents without services. Other parents find themselves troubled by the inaccessibility of their child during work hours. Should a child become ill there is often time lost in reaching the day care site. By contrast, the business-sponsored program has hours and day of operation coinciding with worker needs, and the child and parent are always near

---

[7]Ibid.

[8]Employers and Child Care: Establishing Services Through the Workplace. Washington, DC: U.S. Department of Labor, Women's Bureau, January 1981, pp. 6-8.

one another. Many on-site programs welcome parents at lunch
and breaktimes to share a meal or activity with their children. In a very real and positive sense, work and home life
are combined in these centers.

However, the cost of providing on-site day care can be
prohibitive, as is evidenced by the list of centers who have
made the financial commitment. It reads somewhat like the
list of Fortune 500 companies, and includes American Telephone and Telegraph, I.B.M., Procter & Gamble, and CBS.

Despite the desirability of on-site care, and the increase in numbers of working parents needing services, it
seems unlikely that there will be large numbers of employer-
sponsored programs in the future. In addition to the financial aspect of operating a day care center there is the
commitment required to ensure the success of a high quality
program. Many employers, including hospitals and institutions of higher learning, do not feel that providing child
care is a part of their responsibility. Tax laws affective
in 1987 will also have an effect on employers considering new
worker benefits. It must also be considered that the vast
majority of Americans are employed in small businesses where
establishing a day care center is not even a remote consideration.

Instead, it is likely that subsidized child care will
increasingly be available as one optional benefit available
to working parents. Child care assistance may come in the

form of referrals to existing programs, centers and family day care homes. Another option is for employers to pay a portion of the fee for services utilized by parents. In a few select situations employers provide trained caregivers to care for the sick children of workers.

Ultimately, flexible work schedules, opportunities for working at home, and part-time employment will probably provide solutions for the greatest numbers of working parents. Despite abundant lip-service from business leaders regarding the importance of workers' needs, child care is not on the same rung of the corporate ladder with profits.

In spite of recent efforts by the business and industry the absence of low-cost, quality care continues to be a growing concern with millions of children in need of services. Churches, community groups, and schools have begun to address the need for day care programs. Private individuals, at an ever-increasing rate, are going into the business of day care. But even with the extremely low salaries most caregivers accept, the cost of care is skyrocketing, and many parents cannot afford to pay the full cost for child care services. Without federal, state, or corporate subsidies many parents must select cheaper, low-quality alternatives to center-based care for their children.

Many believe that at least some of the answers to this dilemma lie in family day care. Without the high overhead and salaries attached to center-based programs, home-based care is an affordable alternative for many parents. The individualized attention possible in family day care is also favored by many parents of young children. Family day care is, however, also the victim of some of the same problems facing those offering care in other settings. Home-based centers are less regulated in most states than center care, and caregivers are generally less prepared for their work through training and education. It has been abundantly clear for many years that if family day care is to be a viable and effective alternative, many changes must take place in the near future.

Some communities have undertaken unique responses to the funding crisis. In 1985, for example, the San Francisco Board of Supervisors imposed a fee of $1 per square foot of renovated or new business sites in excess of 50,000 square feet. Estimates are that this ruling will raise $1,000,000 per year for day care services in the city of San Francisco.[9] Other innovative responses to the need for child care are urgently needed.

In the last five years an entirely new wrinkle has developed in the funding crunch. This problem concerns the securing of the liability insurance required for most child care programs by states' laws.[10] Few Americans have been

---

[9]Child Care Information Exchange, November 1985, p. 17.

[10]Jim Strickland and Roger Neugebauer, "Yes We Have No Insurance: A Bad Problem Getting Worse," Child Care Information Exchange, July 1985, pp. 26-30.

untouched by the sharp rise in insurance premiums, due, says the insurance industry, to the overall increase in liability litigation. Day care centers have been hard hit by this problem. Some programs have experienced premium increases of hundreds of percentage points or have even been unable to secure a policy underwriter. This problem is even more startling in light of the industry's own revelation that few claims are made against day care centers.

There have been at least two large-scale responses to the liability insurance dilemma, one instituted by the Child Care Action Campaign, the other by the National Association for the Education of Young Children. Both of the efforts have met with problems, the former being resistance from state insurance commissioners, the latter including limits on amount of coverage and certain exemptions. While efforts by the Reagan administration to limit liability awards may eventually bring rates down, many centers are in crisis in the present.

One of the issues most frequently raised in the past twenty-five years concerns the effects of day care and other preschool programs on young children. Children in Head Start and other programs have been followed longitudinally since the 1960s to determine the impact out-of-home care has on various aspects of development. The first studies of the effects of early childhood programs centered largely around cognitive growth. It was hoped that preschool-educated children would demonstrate significantly higher levels of academic achievement than non-preschool groups, but the early studies were disappointing. It was found that by third grade those children with preschool experience were virtually indistinguishable, from an academic standpoint, from those reared entirely at home. Subsequent research has focused more upon other aspects of development, and these results have been more encouraging.

Research on Head Start graduates conducted by the High/Scope Educational Research Foundation uncovered results of preschool experience that fall into both cognitive and social-emotional realms.[11] Children who attended preschool were found to be more likely to complete high school and secure post-secondary training or education. These youngsters were less likely to require special education or be labeled "delinquent." Researchers concluded that four dollars were saved for every one dollar invested in quality preschool education programs.

Michael Rutter, of the Institute of Psychiatry, University of London, compared the results of research on the

---

[11]Suzanne Guinzburg, "Head Start Makes Sense," Psychology Today, February 1984, p. 10.

effects of day care.[12] While he stressed the importance of
factors such as the child's age at the time of entry into
substitute care, degree of trust established between child
and caregiver, family stability, and ratio of day care staff
to children, Rutter concluded that quality day care does not
harm children's social-emotional growth. Although some
studies have found day care children to be more aggressive
than those reared entirely at home,[13] Rutter disagrees. He
suggests that family influence is a greater factor in the
development of aggression.

A continuing issue, seemingly far from resolution, concerns the components of quality care. While professional
organizations and their journals have consistently written
about the caregiving factor as the key to high quality programs, there have been new and conflicting elements introduced into the day care community. One of these is the
increased demand of parents for a strong educational or
learning component designed to build academic skills. The
other is the increase in the numbers of unlicensed programs,
some of which emphasize the child care setting and equipment

---

[12]Michael Rutter, "Social-Emotional Consequences of Day
Care for Preschool Children," In E. F. Zigler and E. W. Gor-
don. Day Care: Scientific and Policy Issues. Boston:
Auburn House, 1982.

[13]Elizabeth Stark, "Day Care and Aggressiveness,"
Psychology Today, January 1986, p. 68.

rather than the appropriateness of adult-child interactions. These influences have counteracted those values and aspects of day care the profession has attempted to stress, while muddling public perceptions of the important aspects of day care. Clearly, additional public education and caregiver training are needed if there is ever to be agreement on the components of quality care.

Questions have also been repeatedly raised about who should bear responsibility for the quality of programs. Some suggest the providers must be the monitors. That is, those most aware of what constitutes quality care should be responsible for assuring it occurs. The Center Accreditation Program established by the National Association for the Education of Young Children is one way of assessing the quality of programs. Others suggest that quality programming should not be voluntary in nature. If we mandate certain standards be observed by restaurants and other providers of non-essential services, should we fail to require them for programs serving young children? While this seems a reasonable argument, it is given little attention in audiences other than those composed of day care and early childhood educators. Certainly, unless parents become educated and demanding consummers-of-services, little is likely to change.

This leads us to discussion of policies affecting children and families. As a nation, we have continually

demonstrated the low priority placed on family needs. Consistently, in recent years, legislation to provide better
health care, day care, education, and recreation programs has
failed to pass both Houses of Congress or has been vetoed by
a president. As a group, Americans appear to be apathetic
about many issues unless directly faced with them or involved
at some specific level. While the need for child care alternatives is impacting on many families, few are involved in
advocating for them. Instead, the lead has been taken by
professionals working to address family needs. One example
of current legislation is the Parental and Medical Leave Act
of 1986 (H.R. 4300) designed to provide 18 weeks unpaid leave
to parents for the care of an ill, newborn, or adopted
child.[14] While such measures, if adopted, will not change
a families long-term need for child care, they would provide
time for the all-important acquaintance-attachment process
to get underway and relieve the guilt experienced by many
parents who must leave their newborns in the first weeks of
life in order to retain their positions at places of employment. In addition, increased tax incentives for business-
sponsored day care programs and even government-sponsored
advisory centers for persons seeking program development
assistance would emphasize federal concern for family needs.

---

[14]Report on Preschool Programs, Vol. 18, No. 7, April 2,
1986.

Those who fear for the future of America's children may well be justified in their concern. Not because more and more mothers are working. Not because increasing numbers of children receive alternative care during their parents' business hours. Instead, concern should stem from the lack of policies to assure the safety and well-being of youngsters while their parents are absent from home. The danger lies in the national apathy toward children left alone at an early age to care for themselves or growing up in inadequate substitute care situations. These children may never develop the sense of basic trust in loving caregivers which promotes the growth of independence, autonomy, and self-worth. If in the near future child and family needs are not responded to, our youngsters may well lack the ability or opportunity to constructively contribute to society.

BIBLIOGRAPHY

Effects of Day Care

Ainslie, Ricardo C. (Ed.). The Child and the Day Care Set-
    ting: Qualitative Variations and Development. New
    York: Praeger Publishers, 1984.

    Discussions by spokespersons in the field of the ways
in which children and parents are affected by the kinds and
quality of day care. Also discusses the impact of maternal
attitude on infant adjustment to day care.

Barks, Naomi, "How Day Care Children Turn Out," Working
    Mother, October 1982, pp. 82, 97-98.

    Reports on the impact of day care on children. Suggests
that programs that meet child and family needs are not harm-
ful to children. Emphasizes the importance of high quality
programming.

Bruner, Jerome. Under Five in Britain. Ypsilanti, MI:
    High/Scope Press, 1980.

    An overview of the Oxford Preschool Research Project.
The research proposal, hypotheses, and findings are presented
regarding three types of preschool care, nursery schools and
playgroups, full-day child care centers, and caregivers.

Clarke-Stewart, Alison, "What Day Care Forms and Features
    Mean for Children's Development," Paper presented at the
    Meeting of the American Association for the Advancement
    of Science, Los Angeles, CA, May 26-31, 1985.

    Reported findings of a study to examine the effects of
various types of day care on child development. Four forms,
babysitter, family day care, part-time and full-time nursery
programs were included in this research. While day care had
some impact it was found to be only one of several factors
influencing early development.

Collins, Glenn, "Experts Debate Impact of Day Care on Children
    and Society," The New York Times, September 4, 1984.

A review of the drawbacks and benefits of day care as determined by spokespersons and revealed by research results.

Fallows, Deborah, "My Turn: What Day Care Can't Do," <u>News-week</u>, January 10, 1983, p. 8.

The viewpoint of a woman who believes that the family loses a great deal when they must place their children in day care in order to work. Urges understanding of the value of parenting and pushes for legislation to enable working parents to spend more time with their children in the early years of life.

Garland, Caroline, and Stephanie White. <u>Children and Day Nurseries</u>. Ypsilanti, MI: High/Scope Press, 1980.

A study of the effect of policy decisions on adult and child interactions in the day care setting. Observations were made in nine nursery programs in England. The impact of daily routines, management strategies, and human interactions on two-, three-, and four-year-old children are described.

Goodman, Norman, and Joseph Andrews, "Cognitive Development of Children in Family and Group Day Care," <u>American Journal of Orthopsychiatry</u>, Vol. 51, No. 2, April 1981, pp. 271-284.

Discusses the results of a study which examined the effects of program structure and program delivery system on the cognitive development of preschool age children. Those youngsters who participated in a program with an added educational component, those in family day care, showed greater enhancement of cognitive skills than those in group day care.

Howes, Carollee. <u>Keeping Current in Child Care Research: An Annotated Bibliography</u>. Washington, DC: National Association for the Education of Young Children, 1986.

Information on a wide range of publications in the field regarding the impact on children and families of child care programs. Helpful to professors, administrators, and other child advocates.

Magnet, Myron, "What Mass-Produced Child Care Is Producing," <u>Fortune Magazine</u>, November 28, 1983, pp. 157-158, 162, 166, 170, 174.

Describes the operations of Kinder-Care Learning Centers Inc. Asks what the impact of day care is on the very young child. Ends by suggesting that corporate-sponsored, on-site day care can be beneficial to families and employers.

"School-Based Child Care Programs May Be Wrong for Black Children," Report on Education Research, January 29, 1986, p. 8.

Provides an overview of the report prepared by the National Black Child Development Institute on the participation by black children in public school-based day care programs. Citing the poor record of the American public school system where black children are concerned, the report expresses concern for the probable use of non-early childhood trained teachers in these settings. Teachers in public-school programs for young children are urged to have appropriate training in child development and preschool education.

Gamble, T. J. and E. F. Zigler, "Effects of Infant Day Care: Another Look at the Evidence," American Journal of Orthopsychiatry, Vol. 56, No. 1, January 1986, pp. 26-42.

A review of the research regarding the effects of day care on infant attachment and social-emotional development. Suggests the need for alternatives to day care for working parents of young children.

Funding of Day Care

Child Care: The States' Response, A Survey of State Child Care Policies 1983-1984. Washington, DC: Children's Defense Fund, 1984.

Presents results of the states' response to federal cut-backs in day care funding. The impact of loss of funds on licensing, training, and other program components is discussed. Offers solutions to the child care problem.

Children and Federal Child Care Cuts: A National Survey of the Impact of Federal Title XX Cuts on State Child Care Systems. Washington, DC: Children's Defense Fund, 1983.

The impact of the Social Services Block Grant on the Title XX day care services offered. Explores the quality, nature, and degree of services currently being provided.

Dodge, Anne Burr, and Dana Friedman Tracy (Eds.). How to Raise
     Money for Kids (Public and Private). Washington, DC:
     Coalition for Children and Youth, 1978.

     Developing proposals, interacting with foundation and
federal government representatives, and using federal publications for the purpose of funding children's programs are
the focuses of this book.

Finn, Matia. Fund Raising for Early Childhood Programs:
     Getting Started and Getting Results. Washington, DC:
     National Association for the Education of Young Chil-
     dren, 1982.

     Creative suggestions for fund raising projects to sup-
port day care and other early childhood education programs.

Flanagan, Joan. The Grass Roots Fundraising Book. St. Paul,
     MN: Contemporary Books, 1982.

     Fund-raising tactics and activities for day care and other
non-profit programs. Fun and simple activities that can be
conducted by inexperienced fund raisers.

Kolben, Nancy, et al. The Day Care Fund: Facilitating Em-
     ployer Support for Child Care. New York: Child Care,
     Inc., 1983.

     Proposes an interesting child care insurance type ap-
proach to employer involvement in day care. This report
provides a rationale and outlines the plan for the "Day Care
Fund."

Strickland, Jim, and Roger Neugebauer, "Yes We Have No Insur-
     ance: A Bad Problem Getting Worse," Child Care Infor-
     mation Exchange, July 1985, pp. 26-30.

     Presents the results of a survey of 1200 child care pro-
viders regarding their ability to obtain adequate insurance
coverage for their programs and participants. Findings showed
significant rate increases for many programs and cancellation
of insurance for family day care providers in some areas.
This article dispells myths about the work of insurance companies and explains how insurance company losses have impacted
on day care and other social service programs.

Warren, Paul B. The Dynamics of Funding: An Educator's
     Guide to Effective Grantsmanship. Boston: Allyn and
     Bacon, Inc., 1980.

Complete guidelines for identifying funding sources,
developing grant proposals, and interacting with grantors.
Information on resources is included.

History of Day Care

Goldsmith, Cornelia. Better Day Care for the Young Child.
    Washington, DC: National Association for the Education
    of Young Children, 1972.

    Interesting exploration of the background and history
of day care in New York City and the involvement of the Department of Health. Provides insights into current views of
and issues in day care including government involvement.

Grotberg, Edith H. (Ed.). 200 Years of Children. Washington,
    DC: U.S. Department of Health, Education, and Welfare,
    Office of Human Development, Office of Child Development,
    1976.

    An amazing overview of the history of childhood in the
United States. Trends in family life, child health, childhood
education, child labor, recreation, literature, child development, and laws pertaining to children are presented. Many
facts are enlightening and bring current policies into perspective.

Steinfels, Margaret O'Brien. Who's Minding the Child? The
    History and Politics of Day Care in America. New York:
    Simon and Schuster, 1972.

    An excellent history of the American day nursery. Pro-
vides insight into the political and social environment around
day care today.

Legal Issues

Frank, Mary (Ed.). Child Care: Emerging Legal Issues. New
    York: Haworth, 1983.

    Discusses the impact of legislative changes impacting on
programs for young children. Issues include the abdication
of the federal government's responsibility for education; new
roles for child welfare agencies; and involvement of lawyers
in the juvenile court system.

Rose, Carol M. Some Emerging Issues in Legal Liability of
Children's Agencies. New York: Child Welfare League
of America, 1979.

Discusses a variety of aspects of the functioning of
child welfare agencies, such as agency-child and agency-parent
relationships, children's rights, child placement, record
keeping procedures and the legal issues involved. An appendix
of cases and relevant statutes is included.

Treadwell, Lujuana Wolfe. The Family Day Care Provider's
Legal Handbook. Oakland, CA: BANANAS Child Care Project, 1980.

Provides for the administrator a frank discussion of the
many legal problems faced by day care programs. Easy to follow advice for persons providing child care services and suggestions for obtaining appropriate legal counsel.

Treadwell, Lujuana Wolfe. Why Child Care Needs Lawyers Now.
San Francisco: Bay Area Child Care Project, 1980.

Discusses reasons that the legal needs of day care centers go unmet and the potential roles of attorneys in day
care. Legal problems that are faced by programs include con-
tracts, licensing and zoning issues, child abuse situations,
taxes, and family law situations.

Day Care: Need and Availability

Adlin, Sheryl. Final Report of the Governor's Day Care
Partnership Project, Report Submitted to Governor
Michael S. Dukekis. Boston: Commonwealth of Massa-
chusetts, January 1985.

An examination and response to the critical need for
day care services in the state of Massachusetts. Reasons
are discussed for the emergence of this need and a rationale
presented for addressing it. Project Report makes specific
recommendations for the role of the state government, such
as development of a statewide network of referral systems;
development of day care centers for state employees, and
promotion of school-age child care programs.

Aries, Philippe, et al., "Children," The Wilson Quarterly, Vol. VI, No. 4, Autumn 1982, pp. 46-85.

A series of articles on children, child rearing and care, the child in the family, and policies affecting children. The impact on children of divorce, working mothers and day care, and television are among the factors discussed.

Bennettes, Leslie, "Parents Find a Wide Variety of Day Care Quality in U.S.," The New York Times, September 3, 1984.

Describes center-based and family day care homes and provides tips on locating quality day care. Discusses serious inconsistencies in day care quality that observers should be attuned to.

Berk, Helene J., and Marc L. Berk, "A Survey of Day Care Centers and their Services for Handicapped Children," Child Care Quarterly, Vol 11, No. 3, Fall 1982, pp. 211-214.

Findings are presented from a survey designed to examine the availability of day care services for exceptional children. Results show that of centers included in the study, financial and staff resources play a large part in willingness to accept handicapped children. In addition, many eligibility requirements for programs precluded the admission of handicapped children, such as toilet training requirements.

Child Care: Beginning a National Initiative. Hearing before the Select Committee on Children, Youth, and Families. House of Representatives, Ninety-Eighth Congress, Second Session, April 4, 1984, Washington, DC: Superintendent of Documents, U.S. Government Printing Office, 1984.

Testimony on range of programs, research findings, trends and policy issues related to the need for day care. Information included on social and demographic changes affecting the need for day care services.

Cook, Jacqueline T. Child Day Care. Oakland, CA: Edmunds Enterprises, 1985.

Examines the crisis created for society as a whole and individual children, parents, and employers created by the lack of quality child care programs. Four parts discuss the historical significance of the day care dilemma, types of programs in operation, program and policy issues, and solutions to current problems.

Diamond, Franna, and Janet Simons. <u>The Child Care Handbook:</u>
    <u>Needs, Programs, and Possibilities</u>. Washington, DC:
    Children's Defense Fund, 1982.

    Provides a rationale and documentation of the need for
child care. Describes 12 model child care programs nationwide
and their implications. Discusses the roles of advocates in
helping to address child care needs with quality, low-cost
programs.

"Improving Child Care Services: What Can Be Done?," Hearings
    before the Select Committee on Children Youth, and Fam-
    ilies, House of Representatives, Ninety-Eighth Congress,
    Second Session, September 5, 6, 1984, Washington, DC:
    Superintendent of Documents, U.S. Government Printing
    Office, 1984.

    Represents a detailed look at child care by a bipartisan
committee. Includes testimony by representatives of human
and health service professions, education, business, and government officials. Specifically examines need and availability of care and predictions for future needs.

Kantrowitz, Barbara, Deborah Witherspoon, Barbara Burgower,
    Diane Weathers, and Janet Huck et al., "A Mother's
    Choice," <u>Newsweek</u>, March 31, 1986, pp. 46-51.

    Changes in family life, particularly women's roles and
child care options, as these are created by the increase in
numbers of working women is the focus of this article. Impact of new roles and caregiving alternatives is discussed.

Klein, Robert D., "Caregiving Arrangements by Employed Women
    with Children Under 1 Year of Age," <u>Developmental Psy-</u>
    <u>chology</u>, Vol. 21, No. 3, May 1985, pp. 403-406.

    Presents data from a survey of 55,000 households nation-
wide to determine the varieties of alternative care utilized
by women with children under age one and the impact of background variables.

Meredith, Dennis, "Day Care: The Nine-to Five Dilemma,"
    <u>Psychology Today</u>, February 1986, pp. 36-44.

    Explores day care options and stresses that individual
children have unique child care needs. Points out that quality day care can have a positive effect on children.

<u>National Directory of Child Care Information and Referral</u>
    <u>Agencies</u>. San Francisco: California Child Care Re-
    source and Referral Network, December 1984.

Lists information and referral agencies for child care services in 40 states and the District of Columbia.

Spedding, Polly. Child Care Notebook. Ithaca, NY: Cornell Cooperative Extension, Cornell University, 1984.

Provides chapters on various types of child care services, family day care, school age child care, the roles in meeting employee needs for child care, and starting a day care center. Sections are reproducible for distribution as needed.

Werner, Emmy E. Child Care: Kith, Kin and Hired Hands. Austin, TX: Pro-Ed, 1984.

Provides an excellent historic and current status overview of alternative caregiving. Siblings, grandparents, relatives, nannies, babysitters, family day care providers, and other caretakers are discussed. Also examines Western caregiving values from sociologic standpoints and compares these with views held elsewhere in the world.

"Who Cares for the Children?," Christian Science Monitor. (Reprints). Boston, MA. Christian Science Monitor, April 28-May 1, 1981.

A series of four articles covering the need for child care and various responses to it, including school-age care, family day care, employer-supported programs, and solutions in other countries.

Day Care in Other Nations

Child Care Programs in Nine Countries. Washington, DC: U.S. Department of Health, Education, and Welfare, Office of Human Development/Office of Child Development, Research and Evaluation Division.

Describes the trends, structure, and support systems which guide the child care programs in Canada, France, Germany, Israel, Poland, Sweden, the United Kingdom, Yugoslavia, and the United States. Goals, eligibility, staffing, and evaluation information are also presented.

Sidel, Ruth. Women and Child Care in China: A Firsthand Report. New York: Penguin Books, Inc., 1974.

An account of the changes in the status of women in China. Focus on the methods of child care and early education, and comparison with these systems as they exist in the Soviet Union and in Israel. Explores implications of Chinese child care for programs in the United States.

Swiniarski, Louise B., "Day Care in Finland: A National Committment." Childhood Education, Vol. 60, No. 3, January/ February 1984, pp. 185-188.

Describes the Finns' national day care policy, programs, and environments in the centers.

Wagner, Marsden, and Mary Wagner. The Danish National Child-Care System. Boulder, CO: Westview Press, 1976.

A description of the child care system in Denmark. Family and group day care services, family support programs, the child care worker training program, and advocacy system are discussed.

Wright, Mary J. A Canadian Approach: Compensatory Education in the Preschool. Ypsilanti, MI: High/Scope Press, 1983.

Presents the findings of studies of the impact of Canada's compensatory education law on low-income children. When this group was compared with children in two other categories, high income-high ability, and low income-average ability, those in the low income-low ability group, as well as all children included in the research were found to have made significant academic gains.

Day Care and the Public Schools

Blank, Helen, "Early Childhood and the Public Schools: An Essential Partnership," Young Children, Vol. 40, No. 4, May 1985, pp. 52-55.

Explores present and potential roles of public school in meeting child care needs of families. Suggests steps to be taken by early childhood educators to maximize potential for center and public school cooperation and involvement.

Caldwell, Bettye M., "Day Care and the Schools," Theory into Practice: Early Education-Child and Context, Vol. XX, No. 2, Spring 1981, pp. 121-129.

An advocacy position for the interaction of day care and public schools. Overview of various models for day care situated in school settings. Deterrents to success of programs are also presented.

Levine, James A. Day Care and the Public Schools: Profiles of Five Communities. Newton, MA: Education Development Center, Inc., 1978.

Provides an overview of the pros and cons of public school sponsorship of day care. Suggests techniques for using public school systems as a resource and site for child care programs.

Quality in Day Care Programs

Blum, Marian. The Day Care Dilemma: Women and Children First. Lexington, MA: Lexington Books, 1983.

Explores some of the most crucial issues facing the day care community and the nation. The low salaries and status of caregivers, staff shortages, potentially negative impact of child care on children and parents are some of this volume's topics.

Butler, Annie L., "A Child's Right to Quality Day Care," A Position Paper. Washington, DC: Association for Childhood Education International, 1970.

Describes the need for quality day care and the types of programs available. Standards for child care licensing and responsibilities of programs are also discussed.

Caldwell, Bettye M., "What Is Quality Child Care?" Young Children, Vol. 39, No. 3, March 1984, pp. 3-8.

Caldwell provides a definition of quality child care and refers to the extensive efforts of the National Academy of Early Childhood Programs and the development of the system for program accreditation. The author also charges professionals in the field with a number of tasks for achieving the goal of public education about the field.

Carter, Margie, "NAEYC's Center Accreditation Project: What's It Like in Real Life?" Child Care Information Exchange, May 1986, pp. 38-41.

A description of the Center Accreditation Program of the National Association for the Education of Young Children and the experiences of those programs who have gone through the accreditation process. Rewards and problems and advice to those who wish to apply.

Collins, Glenn, "U.S. Day Care Guidelines Rekindle Contro-
versy," The New York Times, February 4, 1985.

The focus of this article is that funds aimed at pre-
venting child abuse in day care centers have failed to address the broad concern for higher quality programs.

Lindsey, Robert, "Increased Demand for Day Care Prompts a
Debate on Regulation," The New York Times, September 2,
1984.

Describes concerns related to child abuse, custodial and
educational care, and pressures for higher quality programs.
Explores how various states have legislatively responded to
these issues.

Ruopp, Richard, et al. Children at the Center: Final Report
of the National Day Care Study, Vol. I. Cambridge, MA:
Abt Associates, 1979.

Presents the major findings of the four year study of the
impact of center characteristics on the cost and quality of
care for preschool-age children. Implications for federal day
care policy are discussed. Summary of Infant/Toddler Care
Study is included.

Regulation and Policies for Day Care

"Child Abuse and Day Care," Joint Hearing Before the Subcom-
mittee on Oversight of the Committee on Ways and Means
and Select Committee on Children, Youth, and Families,
House, 98th Congress, 2nd Session, September 17, 1984,
Washington, DC: Superintendent of Documents, U.S. Government Printing Office, 1985.

Hearings aimed at answering two questions: What role
can the federal government play in helping states develop
procedures and standards to minimize occurrence of child
abuse and neglect? How can prompt response be assured when
incidents do occur? Legislators examined the impact of the
transformation of Title XX to Block Grant funding on ability
of the federal government to assure the quality of day care
services.

Collins, Raymond C., "Child Care and the States: The Comparative Licensing Study," Young Children, Vol. 38, No. 5,
July 1983, pp. 3-11.

Summarizes the primary findings of the Ruopp (1979) research, which studied federally funded day care programs and
their impact. The 1981 regulations for day care are surveyed.
Collins points out that although Ruopp identified problems
and made suggestions for change, few of his recommendations
have been acted upon.

Comparative Licensing Study: Profiles of State Day Care
    Licensing Requirements. Washington, DC: Lawrence
    Johnson and Associates, Inc., 1981-1982.

Examines licensing requirements in 50 states for family
day care homes, day care centers, and group day care homes.
Five volumes compare standards on a state-by-state basis.

Families and Child Care: Improving the Options. A Report by
    the Select Committee on Children, Youth and Families.
    U.S. House of Representatives, Ninety-Eighth Congress,
    Second Session, with Additional Views, 1985.

Details findings of year-long investigation and makes
specific recommendations for adoption of policy for day care
by federal government to support and sponsor day care.

Goetz, Elizabeth M., and K. Eileen Allen (Eds.). Early Child-
    hood Education: Special Environmental, Policy, and Legal
    Considerations. Rockville, MD: Aspen Systems Corpora-
    tion, 1983.

Describes the ways in which children and families are
affected by the environmental aspects, political and legal
issues of day care and early childhood education.

Greenblatt, Bernard. Responsibility for Child Care. San
    Francisco: Jossey-Bass, Publishers, 1977.

Analyzes the shift in the policies of the federal government from reliance on child care provided by the family
to that provided by agencies. Those factors which inter-
fered with previous government involvement are discussed.
Types of child care existing before and after 1960 are described.

Gunzenhauser, Nina, and Bettye M. Caldwell (Eds.). Group Care
    for Young Children: Considerations for Child Care and
    Health Professionals, Public Policy Makers and Parents.
    Somerville, NJ: Johnson and Johnson Baby Products Com-
    pany, 1986.

Provides comprehensive coverage of some of the most important issues in day care, including involvement with a variety of family needs, the role of public policy, and corporate involvement in worker needs for day care. Emphasis is also placed on child health concerns as these exist in child care settings.

Haskins, Ron, and Diane Adams (Eds.). <u>Parent Education and Public Policy</u>, (Volume III of Child and Family Policy Series). Norwood, NJ: Ablex Publishing Company, 1983.

The volume examines a number of issues in the area of parent education. The gap between the views of parent program advocates and federal policy makers is described, and past and current legislation for parent programs is surveyed. A history of parent programs is included.

Kamerman, Sheila B., and Alfred J. Kahn. <u>Child Care, Family Benefits, and Working Parents: A Study in Comparative Policy</u>. New York: Columbia University Press, 1981.

Family and work issues in six countries are compared. Discussion of alternative child care, cash benefits for working parents, and other issues is included. Of interest to a multidisciplinary group of health and human service professionals.

Katz, Lilian G. (Ed.). <u>Current Topics in Early Childhood Education</u>, Volume 5. Norwood, NJ: Ablex Publishing Company, 1984.

Topics in this volume are wide ranging but fall into three general categories: curriculum and teaching methods, policy issues, and indirect issues. Of special interest to day care providers are the policy issue articles, one addressing latchkey children, and one focused on employer-supported child care.

Kendall, Earline D., and Lewis H. Walker, "Day Care Licensing: The Eroding Regulations," <u>Child Care Quarterly</u>, Vol. 13, No. 4, Winter 1984, pp. 278-289.

Points out that effectiveness and quality of regulations for child day care centers is being eroded at the state level. Cutbacks in staff of licensing agencies and policies for deregulation and decentralization are cited as problems. The center accreditation program of the National Association for the Education of Young Children is pointed to as one means for responding to this dilemma.

Kilmer, Sally (Ed.). <u>Advances in Early Education and Day Care: A Research Annual</u>, Volume I. Greenwich, CT: JAI Press, 1980.

This volume is designed to provide an update on research and other developments in the early childhood education field, including roles of policy makers, professionals, and parents in promoting high quality programs. First volume in series.

Lehrman, Karen, and Jana Pace. <u>Day Care Regulation: Serving Children or Bureaucrats</u>? Cato Institute Policy Analysis No. 59, Washington, DC: Cato Institute, September 1985.

A study of the barriers to day care created by the licensing processes and new laws designed to prevent incidence of child abuse and neglect. Offers suggestions for alternatives to state regulations, such as parental monitoring of programs.

"Model Child Care Standards Act--Guidance to States to Prevent Child Abuse in Day Care Facilities," Washington, DC: U.S. Department of Health and Human Services, January 1985.

Guidelines are provided to assist states in the prevention of child sexual abuse in day care settings. The findings of the 1981 Comparative Licensing Study are examined. Roles of parents in prevention of abuse are discussed, as well as the impact of staff background checks, staff training, and appropriate staff-child ratios.

<u>Policy Issues in Day Care: Summaries of 21 Papers</u>. Washington, DC: U.S. Department of Health, Education, and Welfare, 1977.

Shorter versions of 21 issue and policy papers written by experts in the day care community. Child health in day care is one example of the topics covered.

Roby, Pamela (Ed.). <u>Child Care--Who Cares? Foreign and Domestic Infant and Early Childhood Development Policies</u>. New York: Basic Books, Inc., 1973.

Addresses failure of the United States to meet child care and development needs of its youngsters. Compares American and foreign governments' child care policies.

Schweinhart, Lawrence J. Early Childhood Development Programs in the Eighties: The National Picture, High/Scope Early Childhood Policy Papers, No. 1. Ypsilanti, MI: High/Scope Educational Research Foundation, 1985.

This report examines demographic data and the corresponding growth of preschool programs in the United States. Federally funded, state funded programs are described, including Head Start, child day care, special needs programs, prekindergarten, and kindergarten programs.

Stevenson, Harold W., and Alberts E. Siegal (Eds.). Child Development Research and Social Policy, Vol. I. Chicago: University of Chicago Press, 1984.

Examines the findings of research on contemporary social issues and the implication of data for the development of social policy. Topics include early screening, child health, children of divorce, children with special needs.

Stonehouse, Anne Willis, and Faye McKay. People Growing: Issues in Day Care. Urbana, IL: ERIC Document Reproduction Service, 1982.

A series of 26 short reports focusing on child care in family day care and center based settings. Intended to provide issues for discussion by staff and parents. Some reports include references to available materials. Cross-referencing to other reports is also provided. Topics include relationships with parents, the role of the director, and day care routines.

Thomas, Carol H. (Ed.). Current Issues in Day Care: Readings and Resources. Phoenix, AZ: The Oryx Press, 1986.

A collection of articles by spokespersons in the child care community. Includes reprints from journals such as Child Care Information Exchange and Young Children. The 19 different articles address topics such as evaluation of programs, business-sponsored child care, and environment and health issues.

Zigler, Edward F., and Edmund W. Gordon (Eds.). Day Care: Scientific and Social Policy Issues. Boston: Auburn House, 1982.

The theory related to, impact of, and future of the day care movement in the United States. Research on the effects of day care and suggestions for development of policy. An important volume updating many issues.

Zigler, Edward F., Sharon Lynn Kagan, and Edgar Klugman
(Eds.). Children, Families and Government: Perspec-
tives on American Social Policy. New York: Cambridge
University Press, 1984.

With input from spokespersons in child and family services, the editors of this volume explore the impact of changes
in the socioeconomic status of the nation on children and
families. The development of social policy to address child
day care, child health and other issues is also addressed.

Sponsorship of Day Care

Blank, Helen, and Amy Wilkins. Child Care: Whose Priority?
A State Child Care Fact Book. Washington, DC: Children's Defense Fund, 1985.

Provides demographic data on working parents and children and a state-by-state accounting of the response via
funds provided, new programs, and other initiatives.

Browne, Angela C., "The Market Sphere: Private Responses to
the Need for Day Care," Child Welfare, Vol. LXIV, No. 4,
July-August 1985, pp. 367-381.

The author describes three responses to the increasing
demand for child day care services: the business-government
partnership to sponsor work-sit programs; non-profit; and
private, profit-making day care centers.

Burud, Sandra L., Pamela R. Aschbacher, and Jacquelyn
McCroskey. Employer-Supported Child Care. Boston:
Auburn House, 1984.

Presents the findings of a study of 415 operating
business-sponsored day care centers conducted by the
National Employer-Supported Child Care Project. Discusses
the critical need for child care services among members of
the work force and the role of employers in responding to
this need.

"Child Care: Exploring Private and Public Sector Approaches," Hearing Before the Select Committee on
Children, Youth, and Families, House, 98th Congress,
2nd Session, May 21, 1984, Washington, DC: Superintendent of Documents, U.S. Government Printing Office,
1984.

Describes this committee's exploration of the "entire range" of child care issues in order to make recommendations to Congress. Testimony by corporate representatives and others regarding innovative child care alternatives is provided.

Dimidjian, Victoria Jean, and Mary Ann Huizdos, "Designing and Assessing Day Care Environments in Hospital Settings," Day Care and Early Education. Vol. 10, No. 2, Winter 1982, pp. 10-13.

Suggestions for setting up hospital-based day care via transformation of the hospital environment. Sample floor plan is included.

Earl, John H., Jr., and Jonathan B. Wright, "Babysitting--Good for Business," Management World, Vol. 15, No. 2, February 1986, pp. 11-13.

Describes the increasing involvement of corporations in child care and other family support alternatives. Examples of the benefits to business of investment are provided through description of the on-site day care program of Nyloncraft, Inc., Mishawaka, Indiana.

Employers and Child Day Care: Establishing Services Through the Workplace, Revised Edition. Washington, DC: Superintendent of Documents, U.S. Government Printing Office, 1982.

Information to enable employers to plan and implement day care services in business and industry. Discussion is included on funding sources, tax issues, and operating programs are listed by state.

Fooner, Andrea, "Who's Minding the Kids?," Working Woman, May 1982, pp. 99-102.

Describes the growing involvement of the business and corporate communities in the provision of day care for their employees. Discusses benefits to employers in areas of increased productivity, reduced absence and turnover of personnel. Provides suggestions for starting a business-sponsored day care program.

Friedman, Dana. Encouraging Employer Support to Working Parents: Community Strategies for Change. New York: Center for Public Advocacy, 1983.

Reports the results of research aimed at learning about employer responses to family needs. Interviews were conducted in more than 70 cities in order to collect data. Contains a section dealing with obstacles to better employer support of families.

Helping Churches Mind the Children: A Guide for Church-
Housed Child Day Care Programs. New York: Carnegie
Corporation, Ford Foundation, Foundation for Child
Development, 1984.

Designed to provide clergy, church members, and parents with information about the role of churches as day care providers. Discusses four steps to be taken to assess the quality of church-sponsored day care, as well as steps to follow in starting a program. Issues in church-involvement are reviewed. Active communication between churches and the day care communication is urged.

Kantrowitz, Barbara, Diane Weathers, Shawn Doherty, Sid
Atkins, "Changes in the Workplace," Newsweek, March 31,
1986, p. 57.

Corporate sponsorship of day care is described. Discusses possible ways to address unmet and future needs of families.

Linder, Eileen W., Mary C. Mattis, and June R. Rogers. When
Churches Mind the Children: A Study of Day Care in
Local Parishes. Ypsilanti, MI: High/Scope, 1983.

A survey of an initial 87,500 churches and follow up of 3,500 individual programs. Myths about church-sponsored day care are exposed. It is pointed out that many in the child care profession are unfamiliar with the degree to which churches are involved in meeting day care needs.

Mason, Jan, "Child Care Is a Growing Concern: Corporate
Kids," Life Magazine, April 1986, pp. 67-72.

The new role of the employer as babysitter via the corporate-sponsored day care program is discussed. Describes several successfully-operating programs, and the positive re-actions of parents utilizing services.

Meyers, William, "Child Care Finds a Champion in the Corporation," The New York Times, August 4, 1985.

Points out that although there is an increase in corporate-sponsored day care, many executives are still reluctant to provide non-health related family benefits.

Perry, Kathryn Senn. Employers and Child Care: Establishing Services through the Workplace. Washington, DC: Women's Bureau, 1982.

Describes business' responsibility for child care. Discussion of major issues involved in employer-sponsored day care, and approaches to be taken by employees who would like to see a program started.

Robinson, Braxton W., "The Hospital Child Care Phenomenon," Day Care and Early Education, Vol. 10, No. 3, Spring 1983, pp. 28-33.

An overview of the hospital-based child care program, including numbers and types of existing programs, costs, and a legislative preview.

RESOURCES FOR DAY CARE PROVIDERS

American Journal Of
Orthopsychiatry
American Orthopsychiatric
Association
49 Sheridan Avenue
Albany, NY   10010

Beginnings: The Magazine for
Teachers of Young Children
P.O. Box 2890
Redmond, WA   98052

Black Child Journal
1426 East 49th Street
Chicago, IL   60615

Building Blocks Child
Care Edition
P.O. Box 31-0
Dundee, IL   60118

Caring for Infants
and Toddlers
Resources for Child
Care Management
Box 669
Summit, NJ   07901

CDF Reports
Children's Defense Fund
P.O. Box 7584
Washington, DC   20044

Center for Parent
Education Newsletters
55 Chapel Street
Newton, MA   02160

Child Care Employee News
Child Care Staff Education
Project
P.O. Box 5603
Berkeley, CA   94705

Child Care Health and
Development
Blackwell Scientific
Publications
P.O. Box 88
Oxford, England

Child Care Information
Exchange
P.O. Box 2890
Redmond, WA   98073

Child Care Information
and Referral
California Child Care
Resource and Referral
Network
320 Judah Street
San Francisco, CA   94122

Child Care Quarterly
Human Sciences Press, Inc.
72 Fifth Avenue
New York, NY   10114-0042

Child Care Resources
Quality Child Care, Inc.
P.O. Box 176
Mound, MN   55364

Child Development
University of Chicago Press
5750 Ellis Avenue
Chicago, IL   60637

Child Welfare
Child Welfare League
of America
67 Irving Place
New York, NY 10003

Childhood Education
Association for Childhood
Education International
3615 Wisconsin Avenue, NW
Washington, DC 20016

Children Today
Superintendent of Documents
U.S. Government Printing Office
Washington, DC 20402

Children's Advocate
Berkeley Children's Services
1017 University Avenue
Berkeley, CA 94710

Day Care and Early Education
Human Sciences Press, Inc.
72 Fifth Avenue
New York, NY 10114-0042

Day Care Information Service
8701 Georgia Avenue, Suite 800
Silver Spring, MD 20910

Day Care U.S.A.
Day Care Information Service
8701 Georgia Avenue
Suite 800
Silver Spring, MD 20910

Developmental Psychology
American Psychological
Association
1200 Seventeenth Street, NW
Washington, DC 20036

Early Child Development
and Care
Gordon and Breach
Promotions Department
1 Park Avenue
New York, NY 10016

Early Child Research
Quarterly
Ablex Publishing Corpo-
ration
355 Chestnut Street
Norwood, NJ 07648

Early Years
P.O. Box 7950
Philadelphia, PA 19101

ECEC
Early Childhood Education
Council of New York City
66 Leroy Street
New York, NY 10014

Ecumenical Child Care
Newsletter
National Council of the
Churches of Christ
475 Riverside Drive
Room 572
New York, NY 10115

Exceptional Children
Council for Exceptional
Children
1920 Association Drive
Reston, VA 22091

Family Resource Coalition
Report
Family Resource Coalition
230 North Michigan Avenue
Suite 1625
Chicago, IL 60601

First Language
Alpha Academic
Half Penny Furge
Mill Lane
Chalfonte Street
Giles, Bucks HP84NR, England

First Teacher
P.O. Box 29
Bridgeport, CT 06602

Gifted Children Newsletter
80 New Bridge Road
P.O. Box 7200
Bergenfield, NJ 07621

Growing Child Research
Review
22 North Second Street
P.O. Box 620
Lafayette, IN 47902

Journal of Children in
Contemporary Society
Haronton Press
28 East 22 Street
New York, NY 10010

Journal of Research in
Childhood Education
Association for Childhood
Education International
11141 Georgia Avenue
Suite 200
Wheaton, MD 20902

Keys to Early Childhood
Education
Capitol Publishers, Inc.
1300 North 17th Street
Arlington, VA 22209

Merrill-Palmer Quarterly
of Behavior and Development
Wayne State University Press
Detroit, MI 48202

Parents Magazine
80 New Bridge Road
Bergenfield, NJ 07621

Parents Resources, Inc.
Box 107
Planetarium Station
New York, New York 10024

Partners in Parenting
Family Focus, Inc.
2300 Green Bay Road
Evanston, IL 60201

Preschool Perspectives
P.O. Box 7525
Bend, OR 97708

Report on Preschool
Education
Capitol Publications, Inc.
1300 North 17th Street
Arlington, VA 22209

SACC Newsletter
Wellesley College
School-Age Child Care
Project
Center for Research on
Women
Wellesley, MA 02181

School Age NOTES
P.O. Box 120674
Nashville, TN 37212

Social Work in Education
National Association of
Social Workers
2 Park Avenue
New York, NY 10016

Topics in Early Childhood
Special Education
Aspen Systems Corporation
1600 Research Blvd.
Rockville, MD 20850

Washington Social
Legislation Bulletin
CWLA Center for Government
Affairs
DuPont Circle Building
1346 Connecticut Avenue, NW
Washington, DC 20036

Working Parents Magazine
441 Lexington Avenue
New York, NY 10017

Young Children
National Association for
Education of Young Children
1834 Connecticut Avenue, NW
Washington, DC 20009

Your Caregiving Self
P.O. Box 393
Pitman, NJ 08071

Zero to Three
National Center for
Clinical Infant Programs
815 15th Street, NW
Suite 600
Washington, DC 20005

AUTHOR INDEX

Cross, M., 58
Cross, R. T., 162
Cruikshank, D. E., 55
Cryer, D., 130

Dail, P. W., 76
Dana, F. T., 181
Day, B., 55, 56, 58
Deal, T., 2, 15
Debelak, M., 56
Decker, C. A., 16
Decker, J. R., 16
Divine-Hawkins, P., 130
Diamond, F., 185
Dimidjian, V. J., 195
Dittman, L., 115, 132
Dodge, A. B., 181
Doherty, S., 196
Dorsey, A. G., 19
Draper, T. W., 34
Drake, K. N., 56
Dreskin, W., 76
Dreskin, W., 76
Driscoll, L. A., 97
Durant, L., Jr., 20, 26, 69, 154, 155, 160

Earl, J. H., Jr., 195
Edgar, E., 80
Eheart, B. K., 117
Elden, B. S. H., 142
Eliason, C. F., 56
Eller, C., 144
Endres, J. B., 56
Endsley, R. C., 76
Escobedo, L. E., 59
Evans, E. B., 115
Eyer, D. W., 116

Fallows, D., 64, 179
Fane, X. F., 33
Fernandez, H. C., 161
Fiarotta, P., 56
Fiene, R. J., 97
Figgures, C., 144
Filstrup, J. M., 77
Finn, M., 181
Fitzgerald, D. L., 55
Flanagan, J., 181
Flatter, C. H., 142
Fooner, A., 69, 195
Fowler, W., 97, 116

Frank, M., 16, 182
Franzell, D., 20
Freudenberger, H., 161
Friedman, D., 195
Frost, J. L., 56
Frye, D., 116
Fugua, R. W., 16

Galinsky, E., 77, 131
Gamble, T. J., 180
Garland, C., 179
Genishi, C., 96, 97
Gerstein, H., 32
Glickman, B. M., 77
Goetz, E. M., 190
Goldman, R., 33
Goldsmith, C., 182
Gonzalez-Mena, J., 116
Good, T. L., 54
Goodman, N., 179
Goodwin, W. L., 97
Gordon, E. W., 193
Gordon, T., 34, 77
Gould, N. P., 34
Greenberg, P., 34
Greenblatt, B., 190
Greenfield, P. M., 116
Greenman, J. T., 16
Griffin, A., 131
Gross, D. W., 77
Grossman, B. D., 16
Grotberg, E. H., 182
Guinzburg, S., 173
Guzenhauser, N., 190

Haas, C. B., 57
Hardy, S. B., 35, 36
Harlan, J., 57
Harms, T., 97
Harrazan, B. L., 17
Harris, M., 129
Hartman, B., 17
Haskins, R., 191
Hatfield, L. M., 98
Hatoff, S., 57
Headley, N., 39
Heasley, C. A., 162
Heller, P. B., 17
Hendrick, J., 40, 57
Herbert-Jackson, E., 116
Hernandez-Logan, C., 34
Herr, J., 56

Hess, R. D., 34, 55, 118
Hewes, D. W., 17
Hildebrand, V., 8, 17
Holt, B. G., 57
Honig, A. S., 44, 77, 98, 105, 108, 117
Hooks, W. H., 131
Horowitz, E. G., 78
Host, M. S., 17
Hostetler, L., 34, 161
Howes, C., 117, 179
Houston, J. P., 59
Houston, V., 148
Huck, J., 185
Huizdos, M. A., 195
Hunnes, B., 14
Hurst, M., 142
Hymes, J. L., Jr., 161
Hyson, M. C., 57

Irwin, D. M., 98

Jackson, B., 35
Jackson, S., 35
Jacobson, M., 56
Jaisinghani, V. T., 131
Jaworski, A. P., 119
Jenkins, L. T., 56
Jensen, L. R., 55
Joffe, C. E., 78
Johnson, S., 78
Jones, E., 117
Jones, L., 35, 153
Jorde, P., 161
Joy, L., 74
Juhasz, A. W., 37

Kagan, S. L., 194
Kahn, A. J., 191
Kaizma, K., 14
Kamerman, S. B., 191
Kamii, C., 58
Kantrowitz, B., 167, 185, 196
Kasindorf, M. E., 35
Katz, L. G., 35, 161, 162, 191
Kearney, S. S., 145
Keister, M. E., 104
Kendall, E. D., 191
Kennell, J. H., 65

Kennedy, A., 2, 15
Kenny, E. M., 162
Keyes, C., 16
Kilmer, S., 117, 192
King, E. W., 19
Kissinger, J. B., 56
Klaus, M. H., 65
Klein, R. D., 185
Klinman, D. G., 78
Klugman, E., 34, 194
Kohl, R., 78
Kolb, S., 145
Kolben, N., 181
Kontos, S., 98
Kostelnik, M., 162
Kuhn, T. S., 150
Kurcher, D., 78
Kyte, K. S., 145

Lally, J. R., 44, 105, 106, 108, 117
Lamb, M. E., 79
Langenbach, M., 58
Langway, L., 103
Lay-Dopyera, J., 36
Lay-Dopyera, M., 36
Leavitt, R. L., 117
Leeper, S. H., 44, 45, 58, 157
Lehrman, K., 192
Lero, D. S., 36
Levine, J. A., 133, 188
Levitan, S. A., 79
Light, R. J., 101
Lingberg, L., 98
Linder, E. W., 196
Lindsey, R., 1, 102, 189
Lombardo, E. F., 18
Lombardo, V. S., 18
Long, L., 145
Long, T., 145
Lubchenco, A., 131
Lurie, R., 118

Machado, J. M., 36
Maize, D. M., 111
Magnet, M., 179
Manburg, A., 61, 79
Margolin, E., 58
Marotz, L., 58
Maslach, C., 16, 154, 162